READING FOR PARENTS

READING FOR PARENTS
How To Help Your Child

by Irene Yates

Piccadilly Press • London

For Tom and Jack

Phototypeset from author's disk by Piccadilly Press.
Printed and bound by Progressive Printing, Leigh-on-Sea, for the publishers Piccadilly Press Ltd.,
5 Castle Road, London NW1 8PR

A catalogue record for this book is available from the British Library

ISBN: 1 85340 327 X

Irene Yates lives in Redditch, Worcs. She was a primary school teacher specialising in literacy skills for 16 years. She is now an educational writer and consultant.

CONTENTS

Forward

1. AN INTRODUCTION TO READING 1-12

2. A LOOK AT READING METHODS 13-25

FORWARD

You are probably aware that reading is an emotive issue, always hitting the headlines.

Schools and teachers are frequently accused of failing their pupils by using 'trendy' teaching methods. Arguments rage between high profile educationalists and politicians about allegedly falling standards.

The press, short of anything else to fill its headline space, crows about 'a crisis in literacy' and rages about 'bringing back' traditional teaching.

What's a parent to believe? And – more important – how is a concerned parent to know what to do?

My book sets out to show you clearly that there really is no mystery to the development of reading skills. I take no sides. I want to explain to you, without bias, how reading works, how it is learned and how you can help your children.

Time after time, research studies have shown that children who learn to read easily and quickly are, more often than not, children from homes where reading is part of the pattern of family life. In other words, reading parents breed reading children. But study shows that this is more likely to do with nurture than with nature. Any parent, given the knowledge and the patience, can create the conditions for switching a child on to reading.

The National Curriculum has imposed its own constraints and requirements upon reading. Many primary schools believe that the teaching of literacy has suffered because the time available for it has shrunk alarmingly.

Whatever the situation in schools is, and however it is eventually resolved, you can't stand back and wait, because while you're waiting, your children are growing and developing – precious time is being lost.

The aim of my book is to answer all the questions you have ever had about reading and to equip you with knowledge that you can put immediately into action.

When you read it, put aside your emotions. Try and forget any treatise you may have read in newspapers and magazines about reading needing to be taught this way or that way and keep your mind open to all the ways that are explained – because what is important is not how reading *should* be taught – but how *your* child *will* learn.

Put aside, also, any prejudices you carry about the way you, yourself, learned to read, as though if it worked for you it must work for your children. As the man sang, 'it ain't necessarily so!' – your children have different experiences, different expectations, different minds from you.

This book attempts to explain reading as it is – simply, without any axe to grind, without any frills. It says 'this is the whole picture of how reading basically works – now, take the jigsaw pieces that are your children and jiggle them about with the ideas and activities until they click into place'.

Keep an open mind, try out all possibilities, sustain interest and, above all, non-judgemental friendly participation.

And watch your children blossom!

Irene Yates, 1996

Chapter One

AN INTRODUCTION TO READING

THE MYSTERY OF LEARNING TO READ

Reading comes very easily to some children, and with a great deal more difficulty to others. The help and support you, as parent, give to your children can make all the difference in the world.

FORGET ABOUT IQ
You might think children who learn to read easily are more intelligent than those who find it difficult. This isn't necessarily true. The kinds of experiences children have in their early years, the way they see themselves mastering reading, and how important or useful they think it is to be able to read, is what will really influence their rate of learning.

HOW DOES READING WORK?
There are many theories and accepted ideas on how reading should be taught, but none of them can be proved. Some of the methods overlap and seem to confirm each other, others are so far apart they're contradictory. The

main theories are discussed in the next chapter.

The only thing that is absolutely certain is that reading involves the brain taking assorted squiggles and marks from a page and turning them into meaningful language.

WHAT ARE THESE SQUIGGLES?

Once a child realises the squiggles on a page are not random sqiggles but are there as useful tools for communication, some of the reading mystique vanishes. Imagine looking at Chinese hieroglyphics or Arabic writing. Unless you've learned the language, it looks like a lot of meaningless marks. This is how a child who can't read sees writing.

If you wanted to, you could make up your own 'reading' language. You could create a whole alphabet or set of words which you could use for your own basic needs such as a shopping list, a reminder pad, a diary. The only problem is, unless other people learned your 'language' they wouldn't be able to communicate with you on paper. And you wouldn't be able to read other people's writing.

This is why we need an accepted set of squiggles that translate into our language.

HOW DO WE DECIPHER THE SQUIGGLES?

When we talk to each other, we use our ears. The clues we are given, in order to understand, are largely to do with sound. These sound clues are called 'auditory'.

When we read, we use our eyes. The clues we are given are to do with looking. These are called 'visual'.

Before children can use any of these clues they need a bank of language or vocabulary that they are familiar with. They can only understand words in print if they have already met them in speech. Think of how, as an adult, you sometimes come across a word in a book that you have never met before. You have to have a 'stab' at pronouncing it, then guess or find out its meaning. Children do almost the same thing when learning to read. They take the visual clues and turn them into auditory clues so that they can try to say the word – but then they use their past experience to search their minds for a word they know that seems to fit its sound and context. The reason children who are profoundly deaf have difficulty in learning to read is that they haven't enough known language to be able to do this.

WHAT DO READERS NEED TO KNOW?

As soon as you realise what happens when you read – turning 'visual' into 'auditory' – some of the skills you need in order to do it become clear. They can all be isolated from each other and developed by themselves, but it's important to realise that they work with each other, as a kind of team, to provide the overall ability to read.

Think of learning to ride a bike. Before you can do it efficiently you have to be able to:

climb on the bike,
balance on the seat,
steer the handlebars,
turn the pedals,
keep upright,
move with speed,
watch where you're going,
– and other things as well.

You can develop each of these skills independently

3

through other activities, and probably you never think that any of them are skills to do particularly with riding a bike. But once you can do them all you can put them together and ride the bike. Not only that, but by practising riding the bike you're actually getting better at each of the skills. Of course, you might fall off a few times. But falling off is also a learning experience. Through falling off you learn what went wrong and what you have to do to stay on!

Learning to read works in much the same way! Children become efficient readers by focusing on each of the skills they need to develop, putting them together – and by falling off and climbing back on for more practice!

It's easy to break down the reading process and isolate some of these skills.

LANGUAGE

If you had no language – if you didn't know words, didn't use them all the time – it wouldn't matter what they sounded like, you wouldn't understand what those sounds meant.

You could give yourself images for concrete objects – you could draw a door, a dog, a desk, for example. But how would you show abstract ideas – how would you explain the word 'idea' if you didn't have the language to do so? The word 'read'? The word 'skill'?

This is another reason why those with hearing impairment encounter problems in learning to read – it is not that they cannot master the squiggles, it is that they haven't enough language to cope with what the words are saying. It's a bit like learning to read in Chinese when you only understand English!

So, as you can see, language has greatest priority.

DIRECTION
When you look at a page, it's important that you focus your eyes in the right place. If you just look at the squiggles as if they're totally random you can't 'read' anything.

There needs to be some control over the marks on the pages – so, in English, in common with most European languages, words go from left to right, across to the end of the line and back to the beginning of the next line; from top to bottom of the page; from the left hand page to the right... And so on, through a whole book or text.

This is called left to right orientation and it's another skill children have to develop.

RECOGNITION
In order for children to recognise the different squiggles which form different letters and words, they have to learn to sort one shape from another. This is called visual discrimination and it's developed over a long period of time.

It's easy for children to fall into the trap of thinking that a squiggle is always the same mark (i.e. makes the same sound) even when it's upside down or back-to-front. After all, a cup is a cup if it's the right way up or not. But letters are different because there just aren't enough ways of making simple squiggles, so some of them are the 'same' but 'different'. A 'b', a 'd' and a 'p' are all basically the same shape but rotated or reversed – and readers have to recognise and remember which sound each of them makes. Hard work sometimes – but there are lots of things you can do to make it easy and fun, as you'll see in the Practical Activities section at the end of this chapter.

ORDER

For children to make any sense of what they're reading they must be sure to read the lines, the words, and the letters or sound units of each word in the right order.

Let me prove it to you:

gtonhni ekam sseen the get lwil fI wgnor in uoy drore snithg.

See? If you get things in the wrong order nothing will make sense!

The skill of getting things into the right order is called sequencing. And it's another skill that is absolutely necessary in order to be able to learn to read easily and effectively.

ALL SKILLS TOGETHER

Children have to get all these skills working together, just as they do when learning to ride a bike. If any one of the skills is a bit lax, then the whole process of reading may become much harder than it needs to be. And once it becomes difficult children tend to think everybody else can do it so why can't they? Then they decide they're no good at it. They inevitably feel it's better not to try at all than to try and fail. They lose interest. The skills they already have get lost. And then they fall off the bike.

Unfortunately, the sad thing about reading is that, usually, as children fall off, they become more and more reluctant to climb back on and have another go.

There's just not the same incentive in reading as there is in cycling!

But you, as parent, have an important part to play in

improving their skills before they fall off – even before they formally begin the process of learning to read. And the more of the skills they develop before they're introduced to the reading process, the easier they will take to reading. The easier they find it, the more they will do. The more they do, the better they will become. The better they become as a reader, the happier they will be in all school situations! This is no exaggeration – the greatest problem that children face in school is reading failure.

This is because what comes with reading failure is a whole baggage of low self-esteem and fear of failure, which infiltrates every aspect of their lives.

LET'S WORK TOWARDS READING

All the skills your children need for learning to read can be developed at home, quite easily. It needn't cost money. It needn't lead to aggravation, irritation, or arguments. Children don't need to know that the games you are playing together are anything to do with reading. In fact, the secret is to keep the activities as low-key as possible, and to make them fun.

Let them be part of a normal day's 'play' activity. Share them with your children and let them see that you enjoy them as much as they do. And remember, the more you stimulate and encourage them, the greater their success when it comes to reading will be.

PRACTICAL ACTIVITIES

LANGUAGE

* Take time to talk with, and listen to, your children. Limit television. Although they're getting some language experience from TV, they're not interacting. They need to be talking as well as listening, expressing opinions, discussing, making explanations. They learn new words by hearing them used in context. If they use wrong words, give the right ones gently. Talk about meanings and explain new words. Point them gently in the right direction. Remember that making mistakes is a valuable part of learning to use the language, so praise them for trying and don't attach any blame to errors.

* Be aware that everything you do – playing games, making cakes, going for a walk – is an opportunity to build up language. Don't attempt to keep up a running commentary but, equally, don't assume your children understand all that's going on without explanation.

* Ask questions, giving them opportunities to put thoughts into words. Give them the chance to explain things to you: 'How do you think the wheels go round?', 'What happens when we water the flowers?', 'Why do we need to put the toys away?'

It really doesn't matter what you talk about, as long as you share lots of conversation. But try not to pretend you're listening when you're not, because children know, and they'll be put off!

* Share books, comics, letters, everything you can find,

with your children, and help them to discuss the pictures/story. Look at mail order catalogues together – point to different objects, name them, and get your children to point them back to you. What do they think is happening in the pictures? Who are the people? What colours can they see? Just talk – and get them talking back to you – about anything and everything.

* Teach nursery rhymes and jingles – the more the better! Sing songs together, make them up together!

* Teach the proper names for everything – it's just as easy to say 'dog' as 'bow wow' and 'dog' is what they'll find in their reading books! By the same token it's just as easy to say 'now put your right arm in your sleeve' as 'now put your other arm in' and they're learning a whole lot more about language!

* Teach 'up', 'down', 'over', 'under', 'behind', 'in front of', and all the 'placing' words you can think of – by playing hide and seek games. Talk about 'back to front' and 'upside down' in any situation they arise – then when you have to explain about 'b's and 'd's they'll know what you mean!

* Play 'Simon Says' and 'I Spy' – make up your own rules and adapt them to increase your children's vocabulary and understanding. You can play them anywhere you happen to be. In *Simon Says* it's just as easy to do 'Simon Says put all the red bricks underneath the coffee table' as 'Simon Says stand on one foot' and there's much more language learning going on!

ORIENTATION

* As you share books, let your finger travel the lines in a left to right direction, so that they get the idea naturally that this is how writing works. Show which way the pages turn, and where on the page the writing starts and ends.

* Do things together – say, 'Let's jump this-away' and then 'Let's jump that-away', so that they get the feel of both directions. You can probably work up to 'Let's start on the right' and 'Let's start on the left', but give it plenty of time and don't push it if it's too difficult!

* Draw and paint patterns together, on paper, in the mud, in sand, on the paving slabs, making sure the hand and eye are travelling in a left to right direction.

* Draw patterns to be traced over and eventually copied. Show the top left hand corner starting point and show the bottom right hand corner finishing point. Make sure they go along each line and back to the beginning of the next one and don't cut any corners!

DISCRIMINATION

* Play lots of 'the same and different' games. Children need loads of experience in this because they need to be quite confident that a chair is a chair is a chair even though one may be an armchair, one a dining room chair, one a high chair (and they can be upside down, back to front etc). But a letter is not the same letter when it is turned round (e.g. 'b' and 'd'). At this stage, don't try to teach letter names because that's not the aim of what you're doing. You are merely trying to get the child to take notice of differences and similarities.

So with the chairs (for example) you can ask 'What's the same about them? What's different about them?'

* Make a set of cards – you only need to use scrap paper and a wax crayon – with pictures and squiggles on them. Start with three flowers which look the same and three cats which look the same. Spread them on the table and ask the children to sort them into two sets. When they're confident to do this, extend the activity a bit. Make six cats, two exactly the same and four different. Ask them to pick out the ones that are the same.

Gradually make this game more difficult. When they have lots of confidence, try working with different letters. At this point they will only be squiggles on the cards, don't worry about naming them, but if they show real interest give them the letters of their name.

The letters that cause most difficulty because they are so similar to each other are 'n', 'u' ,'h' and 'y'; 'm' and 'w'; 'b', 'd', 'p' and 'q'.

Capital letters are not such a problem because even if you turn them round they remain very distinctive. But remember, that most reading is done in 'lower case' letters.

RECOGNITION
* Cut out pictures from mail order catalogues and scatter them on the table. Ask them to pick out particular things, eg. shoes, bicycle, cot. This gives practice in two things – reinforcing language skills and getting them to look with observation at small pictures.

If you can get hold of two copies of a magazine or mail order catalogue, cut out pairs of pictures and encourage them to sort and match the partners.

You need to do the same thing with more abstract

'squiggles', so you might, for example, amongst your pairs of pictures have a pair of letters or words. Encourage the children to match them up even though they may not know what they are.

* Do the same matching and sorting game with beads, buttons, shoes, spoons – in short, anything you have in the house which will develop the skill of observing fine details.

SEQUENCING
You can do sequencing with all kinds of things in the house. Your aim is to give the children an idea of what 'putting things in order' might mean.

* You may choose to put things in order of size, for instance. Get tins and jars out of the kitchen cupboard and put them in order with the tallest first, then with the shortest first, or the fattest first.

* You may put things in order of colour – all the red ones, then all the green ones, then all the yellow ones, etc.

* Tell familiar stories and nursery rhymes but mix up the order, get them to decide which bit should be before and which bit should be after. Prompt them with questions like 'Which bit comes next?', 'Where should I start?', 'What happens at the end?' The ideas of before, after, next, beginning, end, etc. are important concepts for children to understand.

Chapter Two

A LOOK AT READING METHODS

WHAT ARE READING METHODS?

Reading is a complex activity which develops very gradually. Even though your children may become literate at an early age, everything they read and write will add to their ability.

Reading is called a 'cognitive' skill because it happens in the brain. You want your children to learn how to do it for themselves but first they need to be shown how. This is where 'reading methods' come in. They are the strategies reading teachers use to help children learn to read.

WHOLE LANGUAGE
There are several approaches which come under the umbrella of this method, including:

Apprenticeship Reading
Real Books
Language Experience
Context Support
Holistic Language
(See Glossary, for an explanation of these terms.)

Although they may adopt some strategies which are different from each other, they have in common the basic principle that children soak up and use as much language as you give them. The more you give them, the more they learn to use it, in speaking and listening, and in reading and writing.

The more language they use, the more they learn. The more they learn, the more they use. They are encouraged to become fluent readers by using their own knowledge of life and language to give meaning to what they are reading and writing.

In any of these whole language approaches the child is always reading for meaning.

PHONICS

Phonics is a more traditional way of teaching reading. The method concentrates on breaking the word down into its smallest units – letters and their sounds.

It is based on the belief that children learn to associate printed letters with the speech sounds they represent and then blend them together to pronounce a word.

Children are given 'word attack' skills. The aim is for them to 'crack the code' of written words by remembering the sounds for each squiggle, or group of squiggles, and blending those sounds together to form words. This practice is called 'sounding out'.

In Phonics teaching the child is always learning by rote (i.e. practising and remembering) and is not really concerned with understanding.

LOOK AND SAY

The Look and Say method is sometimes called the Whole Word method. Its theory is that children learn to read by recognising and remembering individual whole words.

Words are written on 'flashcards'. The children start with a small number of words, which they practise over and over again in different ways until they have become familiar with them.

The aim of the Look and Say method is for children to build up a whole bank of words which they can recognise instantly, therefore 'read'.

In Look and Say the children are always taught individual words before they meet them in text. Usually they will not be given a 'reading book' until the teacher is sure they know all the words that appear in it. This gives them a feeling of 'instant success'.

WHAT MAKES THESE METHODS WORK?

Most schools today are aware of all methods, resources and current research. They also recognise that different methods suit different children at different times. Enlightened teachers are willing to try out various methods with children who seem not to be achieving as well as they should.

But reading methods are really only part of the picture. A teacher's conviction and enthusiasm have a lot to do with the way children learn. A spirited teacher who instils confidence in her pupils can probably make any method work. On the other hand, an uninspiring teacher can have the brightest children plodding along unresponsively, even though she uses the same methods.

The child's attitude and pre-school experience counts for a great deal. For some children reading is the key that opens a magic door. For others, it may be a battleground, or simply boring.

YOUR HELP IS CRUCIAL

Your attitude towards books and reading will colour your children's. If they see that reading is a pleasurable and important activity for you, then it will become the same for them. On the other hand, if you treat it as a chore or as an unpleasant task – something to be conquered or left until there is 'spare time' – then that is how they will view reading too and it may become a source of difficulty for them.

Your children's earliest experiences of reading will influence the whole of their reading development, so the more enjoyable and rewarding you make them, the greater incentive you will give them to learn to read.

Children who believe reading to be exciting and fulfilling, who are confident that they can master it too, will normally learn almost effortlessly.

FITTING IN WITH THE SCHOOL'S APPROACH

Today, parents are actively encouraged to get involved in their children's reading development. In fact, most primary schools welcome interested parents with open arms.

Take every opportunity offered to find out how your school approaches reading. Some schools hold special 'Reading meetings' where you can find out exactly what the school's policy is. Most have bookshop, book club or library times when parents are encouraged to choose books with their children. Parents are sometimes invited into classrooms to share reading with groups of children.

Many schools adopt a policy of sending home notebooks or cards, suggesting activities your child should do with you. You may be asked to write a comment on how well they did. Don't think this is a test of your children's ability – it's merely a strategy to enlist your positive support! The more you enter into the spirit of the exercise the more benefit your children will reap.

If your school doesn't seem to invite you in, ask for an appointment with the teacher. Tell her it is specifically to discuss reading.

If you still feel you aren't offered any encouragement, use your eyes and ears to work out the methods that are being used.

A 'Whole Language' school, for instance, will have plenty of written (by the teacher and by the class) material on its walls. The children will be encouraged to bring home lots of different books to share with you even before they can 'read'. They will be making their own books and doing lots of free reading and writing every single day. There will be labels and messages all over the classroom – 'Whose turn is it to look after the guinea pig?', for example. Given books to 'read' your children will have a good stab at working out what the stories might say from their pictures.

A school whose main method is Phonics teaching will provide the children with exercise sheets where they will fill in beginning and ending sounds of words. They may 'look for' words that sound the same or spend lots of time learning single letters and groups of letters. On the classroom walls will be lots of display material featuring letters of the alphabet, or sets of words beginning with the same sounds (ch, sh, wh, etc). Your children may come home and say things like 'It was "st" day today'.

A school which is using 'Look and Say' will focus on

words which stand alone. The children will play lots of Snap-type word games and each have a tin or box containing the bank of words they can remember and recognise. Your children will bring 'new words' home regularly so that you can help them to learn them.

If your school shows clear signs of all these approaches you may be pretty confident that everything is being done to help your child on the path to reading!

WHERE DOES YOUR CHILD NEED EXTRA SUPPORT?

Despite good resources and good teaching, sometimes children go through 'sticky patches' for no really apparent reason. It's important to realise that in most cases these are only temporary and a little interest and help from you can get them over the hump.

Whole Language – occasionally children who have sailed through the beginning stages and are starting to read quite well, will find themselves at a loss to know how to work out completely unfamiliar words when they can't get them from the sense of the sentence.

This may be because they haven't picked up any 'word attack' skills and lose confidence when they get to a new word they don't know how to tackle. Use the activities in the Phonics section at the end of this chapter to help them.

They may also need to build up a bank of often-used words which they can recognise on sight. Use the activities in the Look and Say section to help them.

Phonics – apart from auditory difficulties which are discussed in Chapter Five, one of the main disadvantages to this method is that children have to concentrate so hard on breaking down the words and trying to sound them out that they can lose any idea of the meaning of the text. If your children continually become frustrated or seem to offer words that are completely nonsensical even though they 'sound out' all right, it means that they are merely 'decoding' and have no understanding of what they are reading. Use the activities in the Whole Language section at the end of this chapter to help them.

Look and Say – again children using this method may have no strategies to work out new words or to predict them from meaning. Use the activities in the Whole Language and Phonics sections to help them.

YOU ARE THERE TO SUPPORT

Remember at all times that your aim is to help and support your children, not to make them feel they are in competition with their peers, or to confuse them. You need, for the children's sake, to keep very positive and build a fun element into all you do.

Occasionally children will become so upset about what they perceive to be their failure that they will simply refuse to work with you, on the grounds that it 'is not what we do in school'. Try to assure them that you are building on the skills they already possess rather than putting them at odds with what happens in the classroom.

If they flatly refuse to cooperate it would be better to forget it until they are of a more open frame of mind, otherwise they may see your intervention as pressure and it will only exacerbate the problem. Try to keep light-hearted about it and continue to read to them, making the sharing of stories as warm and pleasurable as you can.

WORK OUT YOUR OWN APPROACH

Using the following practical activities and building on them where you can, you can easily work out an approach that will be enjoyable and helpful to your children. Mix and match the activities, introducing them as fun games you can play together; don't let them feel you are piling extra 'work' on them to speed their reading development.

Remember, their concentration span may be short, especially in the beginning, and when they've been at school all day. When they've had enough, stop. Five minutes every day is of infinitely more value than an hour once a month!

You can adapt any of these activities to suit the age and interests of your children. For example, a ten-year-old would be far more interested in making a football poster than an alphabet frieze. Use their interests to advantage – if teaching the alphabet is your aim pick out teams and grounds to suit.

PRACTICAL ACTIVITIES

GETTING STARTED

* Introduce story books and nursery rhyme books when your children are babies and toddlers. Get them used to listening to your voice talking and singing to them, and to discussing the pictures together.

* Stories or rhymes which have repeating phrases or familiar names and words will help your children to predict and join in. Give them lots of praise when they know what comes next.

* While you're doing other tasks – ask your children if they can remember a story you've shared and tell it to you. If they miss bits out, help them by saying 'Oh, didn't xyz happen then? Do you remember?'

WHOLE LANGUAGE
* Play lots of 'What comes next?' guessing games when you're reading with them. Stop at different points and ask them to anticipate the next word or action, but always make it fun. If they get it wrong say, 'You could be right but you're not. Have another go!' If their guesses are completely nonsensical ask them to think again whether it could be a real possibility.

* Write letters or messages to family and friends with your children helping you. They can help to choose the words to use; when you have written them read them back to them, so that they begin to understand the connection between reading and writing. Get them to have a go at reading them back to you. If they are remembering rather than recognising them they are on the first step to reading, so give them lots of praise.

* Introduce books without words so that together you follow the pictures and work out what the words would be saying if they were there. The next step is for them to make up the words of the story by themselves.

* Read familiar books together, encouraging your children to join in with any bits they can manage. Give them time to look at the pictures so they help to remind them what the words say.

* If you are reading to them and you feel they want to take over, stop reading and give them plenty of time to have a go.
Be prepared to give only as much input as is necessary. If they get stuck you can:
– help them to remember or predict what the next word might sensibly be
– ask them to see if the pictures might help
– prompt them by giving the first sound of the word
– encourage them to make a sensible guess
– ask them if they know any other word which looks almost the same

* Be positive and supportive in your encouragement. Give lots of praise to increase their confidence. Should they get really stuck don't let them feel it's a problem, simply give the word and carry on.

PHONICS
* Buy magnetic letters to stick to the fridge. You really need a set of capitals and a set of lower case. Concentrate on teaching one letter at a time. Teach both its name (B) and its sound (buh) – for example. Get your children to choose a letter and make a collection of as many things as they can find beginning with that letter.

* Even though you may have commercial copies, make your own alphabet frieze or book, enlisting your children's help at all stages. Let them choose the words and pictures they want to go with their letters. Use a mail order catalogue and cut and stick, rather than draw, to add even more interest.

* Play lots of *I-Spy* games. Make little flashcards with the letters and sounds on and help them to pick the sounds out. Take turns to spy or remember something that begins or ends with that sound. From single letter sounds progress to unit sounds like 'ch', 'st', 'pl', 'str' (there is a full list beginning on page 103).

* Make another set of cards the same and play simple games of Sound Snap, all players calling out the sounds as the cards go down. Anyone who gets the sound wrong loses a point.

* Use your cards to play 'Find the sound'. Take turns. One player gives a word, the other puts down the sound it begins with. If you play this game with more than one child the winner of the point can be the fastest to find the right card. If you are putting down cards as well, always let the children check whether they think you've put down the right one as this helps to reinforce the letters. Vary the game by going for ending sounds and middle sounds.

* Make a set of envelopes labelled with each letter of the alphabet. Cut out pictures from mail order catalogues, magazines, etc, and together sort them into the appropriate envelopes.

* Play 'Let's Shop'. Choose a sound. The first player

then says, 'We're going to the supermarket/car boot sale/school fayre. Let's buy...' and gives as many items as possible beginning with that sound. The second player takes over when the first player runs out of ideas. The winner is the one with the most and chooses the next sound.

* To understand how phonics works, your children need to be able to break words into syllables. Together, clap the syllable patterns of names, actions etc. Play simple 'Give Us a Clue' games. Don't be frightened to introduce the word 'syllable' – just explain that syllables make patterns in words and use the children's own names and other family names to demonstrate (e.g. clap once for Kate, three times for Christopher).

WHOLE WORDS
* Use a story or rhyme that your children know well. Help them to choose some words (three or four would be plenty to start with) that they know come into the story (e.g. Humpty, sat, wall, fell etc). Write each word clearly on a separate flashcard.

* Teach the words. Show each flashcard as you say the word clearly. Your children should look at the card and say the word several times. Mix the cards up. Say, 'Find the card which says Humpty,' etc. When you think they know the words, say the rhyme together. When you come to one of the words, instead of saying it, they should look for the card. Give lots of praise every time they are right.

Play this game several times a day just for a few minutes. As they get to know the words, add more, then move on to a different rhyme or story.

* Label interesting pictures to go on the wall. You need large, clear poster-type pictures. They should give you the words (e.g. sky, tree, dog, baby) and you should write them clearly in front of them and stick them in the appropriate places together. Talk about the words several times. Use Blu-tak so that you can take the labels off the picture, mix them up and get the children to sort them to stick on again.

* Make shopping lists together, help them to read the words with you.

* Draw and write your own books together. They don't have to be sophisticated formats – you can use any bits of paper and coloured pencils. The important thing is to choose the words together and let them see you writing them. If they want to 'write' them too, encourage them. Accept that they might 'scribble' write, or try to copy your writing. These are two different, but very important, stages of writing development. Staple or sellotape the pages together, write your names on the front as authors, and read the book with them as often as they will.

* Out of the home, point out familiar labels and landmarks together. Most children today can read the letter 'M' which stands for McDonalds! Help them to recognise and remember other word signs.

Chapter Three

A Look at Reading Schemes

What Are Reading Schemes?

You may have heard the phrase 'real books' and wondered what it means – after all aren't all books real? The term simply separates the books which you can generally buy in a shop from those mainly available to schools directly from publishers, which are exclusively produced as reading schemes.

Reading schemes are sets of books specially written with the sole aim of being used to teach children to read.

They are usually designed to fit specific reading methods and the most striking thing about them is that they are clearly graded according to their difficulty, so that they have to be read in a strict sequence.

The early books in a reading scheme try to restrict and repeat vocabulary so that learners get lots of repetition and reinforcement to familiarise them with the words. Unfortunately this means that often the language is stilted and the stories very weak because it's difficult to write a story that really comes alive in very few words.

WHY ARE READING SCHEMES USED?

Although it's expensive to set up a reading scheme in a school it's still very much cheaper to buy whole sets of mass-produced texts from a publisher than to buy enough individual real books from a bookseller to build a complete reading library for a classroom.

Classrooms need multiple copies so that each child who's at a certain level can read the books simultaneously and also so that they can read in groups. You can see how expensive it would be to equip a classroom with books from a bookshop!

Reading schemes make it much easier for a teacher to keep track of all the reading each pupil does. The teacher can mark down the pages of each book on cards or record sheets and tick them off as each individual reads them, then direct them to the 'next' book when it is finished. The teacher can refer to the children's records at any point in time and, because he or she knows the reading scheme books so well, can assess exactly where each child is in terms of reading development. In contrast, trying to keep tabs on a whole library of books which all have different readability (see Glossary) levels, a classroom full of pupils, what they are reading, and which book to give them next, is extremely difficult!

Once a school has chosen a scheme, it will normally supply each class with several copies of the books that fit the age group. The children will progress through the familiar reading scheme as they move from one class to another throughout the school. Each year's teacher knows more or less what to expect from a pupil because they can ascertain what level they're at on the reading scheme.

WHAT ARE THE GOOD POINTS?

Because they take the children through a series of carefully graded steps, reading scheme books can instil a great deal of reading confidence in beginning readers.

The new generation reading schemes are much more fun than the old ones. They are bright and cheerful with lots of colourful illustration. They tend to be everyday family stories which beg children to identify and empathise with the characters. They attempt to 'hook' them in a way the old style reading schemes (Ladybird, Janet & John, Dick & Dora, Wide Range Readers, etc.) never did.

The old reading schemes used to be tied to a particular method of teaching, i.e. Phonics or Look and Say. The stories in a Phonics scheme would repeat sounds: 'Red hen set ten in the pen'. Those in a Look and Say scheme repeated words: 'See Jack. See Jill. See the cat. See them. Jack sees Jill. Jill sees the cat'.

Although these schemes had plenty of repetition and applied a particular method, the stories didn't really make a lot of sense. The language they used wasn't that of real life.

The newest schemes take into account all our current understanding of the reading process. They use far more natural language and are often designed to appeal to the reader's sense of humour in order to make them want to read.

WHAT ARE THE DRAWBACKS?

The two greatest drawbacks to reading schemes are really in the nature of the beast:

1. The first disadvantage is that they tend to foster competition amongst readers. You may think that competition is not a bad thing and in some ways it isn't.

However, children who want to 'beat' their peers will often take a hop, skip and a jump to get to their end product – in this case the end of a set of books – and skim the surface so that they actually miss out on the reinforcement of necessary skills.

Also, children can always see which books other children are 'on' so any child who is feeling a sense of failure will have that feeling heightened. Don't disregard the power some children have to lower the self-esteem of others – 'I'm on Book Six and you're only on Book Two. You can't read!' – and don't underestimate the influence this can have on a child's development. Peer influence can actually make children feel they're hopeless. What they believe about themselves is what they will become.

2. The second drawback to reading schemes is that, no matter how well designed they are, they still tend to be a very narrow path which it is quite possible for children to follow without ever getting off.

Children tend to substitute getting through the reading scheme for reading. They measure success in terms of moving from one book to the next. There is always the potential for a child to gobble up the whole of a familiar reading scheme fluently and still be totally unable to read anything that does not belong to the scheme.

You can also add to obstacles, the boredom factor. Reading incessantly about a particular family and set of friends for the first three or four years of school is fine if your child is absorbed in them from the outset. But if your child's interests lie and develop in other areas – they may be keen on sports, for example, and not drawn towards fiction at all – then your child would be far better suited to reading reference books that engross them with their information. So, the interests of the early, or emergent, reader are of paramount importance.

INDIVIDUALISED READING

The ideal of schools using other books and reading material alongside reading scheme resources led to the development of a system known as 'Individualised Reading' or 'Colour Coding'.

A wide range of reading schemes, non-fiction books, well-known poetry and story books, were grouped into thirteen different reading levels. Each level was coded with a particular coloured sticker. Thus the children on – say – red level, could pick any book with a red sticker and have a variety of material to choose from.

The advantage is that, although this means the children are still expected to move through grades in sequence, they have access to a much greater range of subject matter and style at any one level. Often the reading scheme is the core of the children's reading and they are directed outside the scheme to books at a consistent level to back up their reading.

The disadvantages of this system are the same as using numbered reading scheme books. Children immediately identify their ability level in comparison with their peers. They tend to see themselves as 'a red' or 'a blue' or 'a green' and not want to venture out of that security net. This means they won't give themselves the opportunity for challenging new reading, and may also be reluctant to return to old favourites which are, as they see it, below their reading level. Yet we know that both of these activities are strategies that fluent readers use all the time.

CONTEMPORARY SCHEMES

THE MOST POPULAR SCHEMES

Without a doubt the most popular of today's schemes is The Oxford Reading Tree. It is the scheme that broke the mould and prepared the way for Longman Reading World, Sunshine Books, The Flying Boot, and others.

These contemporary schemes all use whole language and language experience as their foundation. They attempt to make reading fun, interesting and informative. Their basic aim is to hook the learner's attention so that they will want to read more and more and more.

They are also concerned with presenting a view of the world that is not biased, one which helps to increase an understanding of other people, abilities and cultures. In some ways, because of this, they may occasionally stray a little too far along the path of political correctness for the good of the narrative, but it is the price they have to pay to be seen as ideal reading material. They are a big step forward from the old reading schemes which were mainly about white, middle class, able-bodied people who lived in a sanitised world. They often portrayed stereotypes of race, class and gender, or were even offensive in their portrayal of other ethnic or class groups.

The National Curriculum document for English declares that:

Texts need to reflect the multi-cultural nature of society, including home language and dual-language texts, both in fiction and in non-fiction...Care should be taken to ensure that all these materials and their use reflect the equal opportunities policy of the school and the local education authority.

Publishers and writers work laboriously to make sure their current schemes fit into this clear statement, otherwise they will not find a market in the schools.

BREAKTHROUGH AND LETTERLAND

Some schools use the Breakthrough to Literacy system, or Letterland. Neither of these can be described as schemes, but they aren't exactly methods either.

Breakthrough is really a language experience strategy which combines reading and writing. Briefly, it utilises 120 commonly used words which are printed on small pieces of card. The cards fit into a folder which each child has. They take words from the folder to create a sentence, placing them in a plastic stand in the right order. Then they copy the sentence into their books. Gradually as they learn more words, their stories get longer. They are motivated to read because they have created the story.

The problems with Breakthrough are more to do with

its fiddly nature than anything academic! It's difficult in large classes to keep track of all the bits of card and plastic stands. Also it can become quite tedious for the children to keep copying out their stories.

Because it is a very successful programme for teaching reading and writing, you will often find it used in early classrooms alongside reading schemes and other approaches.

Letterland is a pictogram system which was originally devised thirty years ago as a visual aid for ten/eleven-year-olds who were failing to learn to read. Each letter of the alphabet is given a character, which is drawn into the letter (e.g. Annie Apple for A, the Hairy Hatman for H). The children are taught that each character makes its sound – for example the Hairy Hatman says 'hh, hh, hh'. The system includes story books and worksheets. The characters are engaged in stories which are written specifically to reinforce the children's learning of the alphabet and the sounds of different letters.

Letterland has its own problems. Sometimes the children become so involved with the characters that the real objectives the teacher is concerned with are lost altogether. The stories are quite weak, but because the children like the characters they're locked firmly into their heads, thus an A may always be Annie Apple – it's not unknown for children in comprehensive school who learned Letterland in their primary years, still to refer to the alphabet in this way! Many leading figures in the world of literacy development feel that Letterland does not provide enough of a reading challenge.

WHERE DO YOU FIT IN?

Many parents, anxious about their children's welfare, rush out to buy copies of the school's reading scheme as soon as they know what it is, hoping to give them a head start at school.

What this action does, of course, is strengthen the idea that 'the' reading scheme is what reading is all about and that conquering the reading scheme is what is important.

Think about it for a minute. Although you will be reinforcing the work that your children are doing in the classroom, what you are really doing is giving them exactly the same experience as the teacher is. This can put undue pressure on the learners because they may interpret your action as your not being happy with their performance in school.

It's far better to provide different reading experiences, more varied and more attuned to their own interests and background. You are in the ideal position to be able to do this because you know the children and the life they lead, whereas to the teacher they're only one amongst thirty or more.

TAKE THE BEST AND LOSE THE REST

There's no doubt, and the National Curriculum endorses it, that children need to widen their reading horizons as much as they can in order to develop their full reading potential. If you adopt a mix and match approach, rather than stifling your children with more and more of what they're getting in school, you will be broadening their experience.

No doubt they will bring reading material home for you to 'listen to them read' and you need to go along with this as a matter of course. Don't be tempted to voice disagreement over the reading habits that the school uses because all your contradiction will do is set up a tussle between what the children perceive to be the right (i.e. school-based) thing to do and what you want them to do.

Once they lose confidence in what happens in school you'll find it very difficult to give that confidence back.

Even if you disagree violently with the way the school teaches reading, the most sensible thing to do is to give as much support as you can at home and not let your children see that it worries you. Creating a conflict with the school can, in the long run, only harm them by influencing their attitudes.

Much better to concentrate on making reading at home fun and involve them in choosing and creating their own reading material to supplement whatever they're getting at school.

Practical Activities

WRITE YOUR OWN READING SCHEME

You can begin developing a 'reading scheme' with your children right from their earliest days. All you need is paper or card, black felt pens, and ideas.

For the first book in your series you could just introduce friends and family. You need about six to eight pages – anything more will make the book too long. Write one short sentence only, on each page and try and repeat the words as much as possible. For example, you might write:

Page 1: This is Tom (child's name)

Page 2: This is Tom's Mummy.

Page 3: This is Tom's Daddy.

And so on. Illustrate the pages with clear photographs, or pictures that you or your children could draw.

For the second book, move on to describing the people in book one e.g.

Page 1: Tom has brown hair and blue eyes.

Page 2: Tom's Mummy has brown hair and green eyes.

Page 3: Tom's Daddy has fair hair and blue eyes.

For the third book, take daily family events e.g.

Page 1: On Mondays, Tom goes to playschool.

Page 2: On Tuesdays, Tom stays at home and helps Mummy.

Page 3: On Wednesdays, Tom plays with Charlotte.

For the fourth book, you could write about the kind of food the family eats e.g.

Page 1: Tom likes chips and fish fingers.

Page 2: Mummy likes chips and salad.

Page 3: Daddy likes chips and sausages.

Carry on like this to build up your reading scheme as much as you possibly can until you're writing little stories about all the events that happen in your family and friendship circles. Try and keep the children central to the stories.

Always write in clear print (see how to form letters, page 105), don't join the letters up as it will be confusing when the children get to school. Use capitals for the beginning of sentences and put in the full stops. Write with black felts on white paper for easiest reading. Make the body of each letter at least 10mm high.

Go over and over the story books with your children until they know them off by heart. This knowing and recognising is the first step towards real reading. When they really know the words you can play little games: 'Show me which word says Tom.' 'Which word says chips?' 'What does this word say?' 'Bet you don't know these two words.' 'Bet you can't read this whole sentence!'

Try and make the creation of your reading scheme a really fun pastime that all the family takes part in. Write about interests, hobbies and activities. If you can include family jokes and little surprises, so much the better.

If the children seem to get fed up with the activity, put the books somewhere safe, give the whole thing a rest, and come back to it later.

MAKE FLAP BOOKS
A really easy way of making fun flap books:

1. Take one sheet of A4 paper and fold in half lengthways.

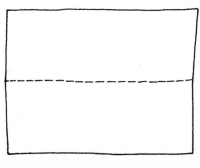

2. Fold it in half again, and then in half again.

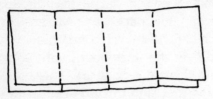

3. Unfold the page, and cut on three folds, but only to the middle of the page.

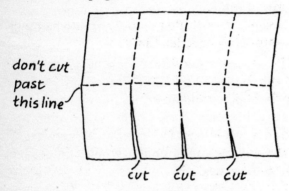

don't cut
past
this line

cut   cut   cut

4. Fold paper in a half lengthways again.

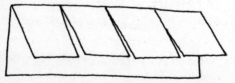

5. Fold into a book and stick back together with sellotape.

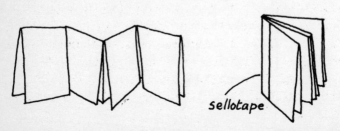

sellotape

Use the flap book to write jokey little stories. For example you might write:

Flap 1: Here's Tom.

  Underneath: Tom says 'Hello!'

Flap 2: Here's Mum.

  Underneath: Mum says 'Hello!'

Flap 3: Here's Dad.

  Underneath: Dad says 'Hello!'

Flap 4: Here's Fluff the cat.

  Underneath: Fluff says 'Mieow!'

This is only a very simple little story, but it's the simplest things that capture early readers' interests.

If the flap books are a success, try using larger sheets of paper. Fix two or more books together to give lots more pages and work out the words together.

MAKE WORD CATALOGUES

One thing children can never have enough of is cutting and sticking. Build up their word recognition skills by helping them make their own word catalogues.

You will need a book or pad, scrapbook size (at least as big as A4, but preferably bigger), some spare card or paper, envelopes, a felt tip pen and an old mail order catalogue. You can make the book/pad yourself with sugar paper. Use two or three sheets, cut them in half, the fold each piece in half to make four sides. This will give you the right size. Stitch or staple the pages down the middle.

Draw a vertical line about two thirds of the way across a page of the book/pad. On the right side of the line stick three pockets made from the ends of envelopes at equal intervals down the page.

Get the children to choose and cut three small pictures from the catalogue. Stick the pictures on the left hand side of the page. Print the name of the picture (e.g. fire engine, baby doll, jeans) on the relevant pocket. Print the name on a small piece of card to fit into the pocket. All your print should be in black felt tip and quite large.

Go over the words and pictures several times. Hold up the appropriate card and say the word clearly. Get the children to look at the print and repeat the word.

Mix the words up. Ask the children to match the printed cards to the printed words on the pockets and place them in the right pocket.

When they can do this easily, make another page. Work on the three words for that particular page. When they know them, mix up the words for both pages and try again. Keep developing this until the children can work on lots of pages. Eventually they will become so familiar with the words they will be able to pick up a card, tell you what it says, look back for the relevant picture and check their suggestion against the word on the pocket.

In checking they will begin to break down the words into letters and units of sound. Help them – say, 'Is the first letter the same? What about the last letter?'

By the time you have filled your scrapbook, you can add other words that would enable the children to work out sentences – you then have your own very simplified version of Breakthrough!

Chapter Four

ENCOURAGING READING

THE READING ENVIRONMENT

Schools pay a lot of attention to providing what they call a 'good reading environment'.

What may appear to you to be a haphazard display of books in a corner is very likely the classroom library. The books are usually placed front-on to the room so that the children can see the covers without having to pick the books out of the stands. This makes it easier for them to choose what they want to read since the colourful covers act as a kind of advert for the book. There will probably be a mat or carpet for the children to sit on or bean bags to lounge on, even an armchair or sofa, if space permits, for the children to sit together.

All of these things are deliberate ploys on the teacher's part to make the reading corner a welcoming and comfortable place.

Every school should also have a central resource library which the children from each class are encouraged to visit frequently and regularly. It should have attractive displays of books and children's writing. Primary schools are often desperate to find parents willing to help with the running of the library so if you think you'd like to get involved don't be afraid to offer your services.

MOTIVATION

More than ever before, children have to be tempted to enjoy the activity of reading. Their leisure time is filled with so many other pursuits they do not naturally turn to books for relaxation, as previous generations did.

Educationalists know that those children who grow up seeing their family read as a matter of course – for information, for recreation, for escape – are inclined from the outset to have good motivation towards reading. They just accept it as a 'normal' thing to do and it follows that they expect to do it too.

Whilst good attitudes are essential, it's not the whole story. Curiosity needs to be stimulated with lots of activities that involve talking and listening, as well as looking at books and practising reading skills.

AWARENESS AND KNOWLEDGE

Right from their earliest days, a tremendous amount of learning takes place when children listen to stories and nursery rhymes. Listening to stories helps children to develop emotionally, socially and intellectually by giving them opportunities to:

* enjoy the rhymes and rhythms of language – they take them on board and use them in their own speech without knowing it

* widen their vocabulary – they hear, understand and use words and phrases that might not be part of their

normal, everyday colloquial pattern

* become emotionally involved – they take the stories to heart, believe in and like the characters

* make sense of their own experiences – by working out how their lives and the characters' reflect each other's

* learn to empathise – they put themselves in the characters' shoes and imagine how they would cope with the same problems

* broaden their imagination by imagining themselves in unfamiliar times, places, cultures

* make a critical response to the narrative – which may begin as whether they like or dislike the story, but will lead towards more structured and analytical criticism

* predict cause and effect – anticipating what could or will happen next

* learn how story is structured – they will begin to have expectations of the rise and fall of story patterns

* add to their knowledge about books – e.g. words such as 'page', 'title' etc.

* understand how print works – e.g. left to right, top to bottom

* learn 'literary' language and style – become aware of the differences between a fairy story, a myth, a contemporary tale, etc.

This is the kind of knowledge that children absorb, simply by listening. They're not really making any effort to learn and only know that they feel satisfied and fulfilled by the exercise of listening and sharing.

LISTENING IS IMPORTANT

Listening experience is crucial to children's reading development. Apart from giving them a much greater ability to understand and process language, it can make all the difference to whether they get off to a good start or struggle when they begin to read at school.

Children who haven't had the chance to build up any of the above knowledge are immediately plunged into a strange and confusing world where the emphasis on books and reading might be quite a threat. They find it difficult to sit still and pay attention for what they see as long sessions. They have problems concentrating because they don't understand why they're supposed to listen, though they may be conscious that others seem to know more than them. They usually view their 'not knowing' as an 'inability to know' rather than a lack of experience. This then convinces them that they are less able, or 'can't read', and builds a huge stumbling block which can quickly get out of hand and turn them into reluctant, or even failing, readers.

On the other hand, those who have built up both the skills of listening, and the bank of awareness they have gleaned from it, move easily and naturally into more structured approaches towards reading.

HOW CAN YOU MIRROR WHAT HAPPENS IN SCHOOL?

The kinds of techniques teachers use to help children become competent readers can easily be modified and made fun at home. The great advantage is that your children can have your concentrated attention whereas, in the classroom, they are always one of many amongst a huge peer group. With you, the potential is there for greater opportunity to learn.

What the teacher does:
* regular storytime sessions. These may take place two or three times during the day, particularly at settling-down periods. The children are often encouraged to choose or bring books they really like for the teacher to share with the class. This gives the whole class a feeling of 'ownership' and 'conspiracy' – almost as though they all belong to a kind of story club.

You can:
Make storytime a regular part of the bedtime pattern, right from baby days. Have different people in the family take part, so that it doesn't always have to be you. Older brothers and sisters are particularly good because it also helps their reading! Make periods two or three times in the week which are always for story. This gets the children used to the idea of routine and anticipation. Storytimes don't have to be long periods – five minutes five times a week is infinitely better than half an hour once a week!

What the teacher does:
* hears children read. The norm used to be for a teacher to attempt to listen to each child in the class read every single day. You only have to work out how many children there are, and how much time is available, to understand that this principle was a flawed one. Far better to listen to a child read a whole story once a week than to listen to two or three lines of a page once a day. More concentrated attention means that the children can get the flow and meaning of a whole story. Before, their reading was often so disjointed it made very little sense to them.

You can:
Make some of your storytimes times when the children read to you. Encourage them to tell the story from the pictures even before they have any idea of the words. Once they have some familiarity with the print, inspire them to 'have a go' at joining in with the reading whenever they can. If they start reading the words, you stop. But be ready to take over again as soon as they reach a stumbling block. Be encouraging rather than judgemental – 'What sound does the word begin with? Can you have a guess at it? Go on... Well done!'

What the teacher does:
* organises quiet reading times. Many schools use a technique called ERIC (Everyone Reading In Class) or USSR (Uninterrupted, Silent, Sustained Reading). The teacher usually acts as a model, reading silently at the same time. The children learn how to select a book for themselves – either because it's by an author they've met before and enjoyed, from its 'blurb' or illustrations, or because it's been recommended. They can try out a page for level of

difficulty, and then settle down to an uninterrupted read. Even before they can read the words they join in this quiet reading time. It all helps them to develop an enthusiasm and love of books.

You can:
Show your children it's important that you can lose yourself in reading material for a short period of time. Get into the habit of buying a weekly magazine for you, comic for them – or get something each from the library. At home, settle down comfortably together for five or ten minutes of uninterrupted reading; no TV, no computers, no visitors, etc. If you do this regularly they will soon get the idea. Again, go for short bursts, not long periods of time which they may find hard to sustain. Try and judge their concentration span and organise the quiet times to suit.

What the teacher does:
* organises paired or group reading. Children join with a partner for regular sessions where they choose, read and discuss a book together. In group reading they usually need to read from a reading scheme to ensure that everyone has the same text which they read together and discuss.

You can:
Encourage your children to read with their friends. You could make books yourself about their activities together. You need only make them very simply but it's guaranteed that if their names appear and *you* have written it, they'll love it!

What the teacher does:
* discussion. Children are encouraged to share the details of stories, events etc. in order to develop the skills of recalling, retelling and sequencing.

You can:
Talk about the children's day. They are notorious at replying 'Nothing' when you ask, 'What did you do today?' so you have to learn to frame the question differently. Try using 'Tell me...' rather than 'What...?' and be specific. 'Tell me what you did at playtime...' 'Tell me what you did in PE...' 'Tell me what Assembly was about...' should get more response.

What the teacher does:
* publishes children's stories. The children are encouraged to use their writing and presentation skills to make books of their own stories or adaptations of what they've read. The books are displayed in an accessible place so that anyone can read them.

You can:
Do the same. Make your own books as models and help your children to create their own. Children find some very special kind of magic in books they have produced themselves and this makes them willing to read them over and over again. They are especially proud if family and friends, when visiting, ask 'Any new books since last time?' and read them avidly.

What the teacher does:
* games (such as those described in Practical Activities throughout this book) to help the children focus on print.

You can:
Choose the games you feel will help your children on their path to fluent reading and play them at opportune moments.

Remember, always, that whichever of these techniques you decide to use (and don't allow yourself to feel so responsible that you try to employ them *all*, all the time!), your enthusiasm will always be the most important factor. Your canon should be that if you really don't feel like it, don't do it! There's no point struggling through a headache to try and listen to your children read just because it's prescribed by routine. You will only be edgy and impatient, and if you don't carry out the activity in a naturally spontaneous manner, your attitude will rub off on them. It really doesn't take a lot to put children off reading. If they get the idea that you're doing it under sufferance then so will they!

DIFFERENT LEVELS OF ABILITY

It's as well to be aware, at this point, that in every reception class (in fact, every class throughout school life) there will be a huge disparity between pupils at different stages of reading development. Teachers are trained to recognise and cope with this differentiation.

There should never be a situation where some children are marking time waiting for others to catch up, nor for a slow learner being left to struggle alone.

If either of these situations occurs with your children, you should arrange to discuss it with the teacher. If no satisfactory explanation is forthcoming, make an appointment to discuss it with the head teacher.

OLDER CHILDREN/RELUCTANT READERS

Apart from when specific problems are present (see Chapter Five), children sometimes, despite all your efforts, may be unwilling to play the reading game.

There's no doubt that the most disinclined readers are boys. Often you can address the problem by completely changing the range of texts you expect them to read. The key factor is to find out what it is that really interests them.

As they get older, many boys seem to grow some kind of aversion towards stories or fiction in any shape or form. On the other hand, they're usually interested in making things, researching projects, playing computer/intellectual games and sports.

As long as they are reading, they are practising their skills no matter what they're reading. So try and provide them with things that capture their imagination. Football programmes, sports magazines, superstar biographies are all good strong reading material. If they have a model to build they don't even know they're reading when they're trying to work out the instructions. Likewise, the rules of a new game can absorb them totally. Looking up TV programmes and searching through teletext for information is also reading. Get them to look up information that you want – e.g. weather forecasts, road conditions, etc.

Try and give them some sort of challenge, where the

end result comes about by reading. This makes the result – information gathering or whatever – the focus of the exercise, rather than the reading itself. In this way they forget they're reading, so they forget to be reluctant.

Where they have younger brothers and sisters, encourage them to help those younger children to read. In this way they'll be doing the activities themselves and developing their own skills, whilst thinking only that they are helping the younger ones.

Girls take to reading as a leisure activity much more readily than boys. They're helped by the huge range of magazines and comics available for them, which they like to share with friends. You might decide that some of this material is a bit suspect in content and that you need to act as a censor. Try and find a balance between how much you want them to practise their reading skills and how little you want them to read the material. The chances are they'll be acquainted with the material through their friendship groups anyway. At least if you're buying it and reading it with them they're not reading it in secret, and you can discuss it with them and decide together what its merits are.

Even teenagers need to practise reading techniques to develop their skills. Often they've been put off by the sheer amount of reading material they have to get through at school and what they see as the monotony of it. If it's exam-orientated it doesn't always seem to have much relevance to their lives. But they're often happy to read music magazines or fanzines, true tales of mystery and amazing experiences, how-to books that tell them how to build a car or work their way around the world on a shoestring. Just because they read it doesn't necessarily mean they'll go out and do it so try to encourage them to widen and broaden their capacity for reading by just dropping a book casually on the sofa for them to pick up, preferably without comment. If they think you want them to read it, they probably won't. If they pick it up and browse, and it fires their imagination, then they probably will!

PRACTICAL ACTIVITIES

BE A GOOD ROLE MODEL

* When you need information, use print to locate the source of what you need to know, and then find that information. Use the TV and radio listings, Yellow Pages, cookery books, reference books, holiday brochures, manuals.

* Read for relaxation and pleasure. Let them see you 'curl up with a good book' as often as you can. Read newspapers and magazines regularly for information and for escape.

* Read as many of your children's books as you can manage, so that you can make a positive response when they discuss them with you.

PRESENT A GOOD READING ENVIRONMENT

* Make newspapers, magazines and books all part of the atmosphere of home, not things to be tidied away and retrieved only at certain times.

* Introduce books to your children as babies. Get hold of lots of different types of book and build up an accessible

library with bath books, board books, pop-ups, reference, picture-story, home-made books etc.

* Be ready to discuss stories or texts with your children, whatever their age. Give them the opportunity to form their own opinions and remember that children need to develop their own tastes so don't try to push them into reading what you enjoy.

CHOOSING BOOKS WITH CHILDREN
* Try to find books that will appeal and add to your children's interests. Consider the reading level by looking at the whole length and the ratio of text to illustrations. A good bookseller or librarian is always available to give you advice on selection – it's part of their job.

JOIN THE LIBRARY
* Make regular visits so that it becomes an accepted part of your children's lives. Allow them to make their own choices. Children like the tried and tested, so don't be discouraged if they seem to be reading the same material over and over again. Just occasionally try to entice them towards something different.

Help them to understand how the library works, and make good use of the children's reference section. Explain how to locate information, how to use the contents pages and indexes, how dictionaries and encyclopedias work. Children who miss this valuable information in school, or who don't understand right away, will find it very difficult to cope and may not like to ask their teacher in case they're thought slow.

Encourage your children to ask the librarian to explain to them how the catalogue system and microfiche work.

HOME EVENTS
* Make as much use of notes and lists as you can. When friends call, make a note to read instead of telling them. Make shopping lists and gardening lists and encourage the children to read them back to you. Let them help to plan holidays and trips; give them brochures to read and information packs to work their way through.

* Bus and rail timetables are excellent reading matter; children make a huge leap forward in comprehension (understanding, see Chapter Seven) skills when they can use them.

* Teach them to read simple maps and street guides.

* Give them opportunities to really use their skills in navigating – this will pose a challenge and make them want to work on more difficult maps.

* On journeys, get them to look out for signs and directions. Play games with car registration letters – e.g. use each letter as an initial to create a phrase or sentence, or try to make up words using the letters as a framework.

Chapter Five

READING DIFFICULTIES

WHEN PROBLEMS ARISE

Just as all children do not grow at the same rate, all children do not learn to read at the same rate. Most children learn to read between the ages of three and eight. Some learn easily, quickly becoming fluent and independent readers. Others find the process more laborious and it may take two or three years for everything to click into place. Each of these circumstances can be considered quite 'normal' and there are wide variations between the two ends of the scale.

As long as your children appear to be making some progress, even if it is slow, there is no need to worry.

If, by the age of seven, there appears to have been no breakthrough whatsoever into the process of reading, you need to do something about it.

Reading difficulties can have many different causes but often, by a process of elimination, you can get to the root of the problem.

In the main, problems will fall into one or more of three areas:

PHYSICAL PROBLEMS

EYESIGHT: Long sight, short sight, astigmatism, squint, excessive blinking.

Children with an eyesight problem often develop compensating techniques so that it remains undetected. After all, they don't realise that other people see differently from them so they learn to cope.

What to watch out for: constantly rubbing eyes; struggling to focus; screwing up eyes; frequent headaches; having difficulty in balancing.

What to do: Request a full optic screening through your GP or the school medical service.

VISUAL DISCOMFORT

When sufferers of visual discomfort look at a page the print may appear to jump, change shape, wobble or blur. Sometimes colours appear and disappear around the letters.

What to watch out for: Complaints of this nature.

What to do: Alert the school and ask for specialist assessment. Colour tinted glasses or coloured plastic overlays often help. (See page 102 for the address of the Irlen Centre.)

HEARING

There are many levels of hearing impairment, any of which will hinder a child's reading ability.

What to watch out for: Unresponsiveness to sound or speech; constantly lost in a world of their own; speech that seems to be unconnected to what's going on; unclear speech; vacant looks when asked or told something. Often children with slight hearing impairments learn to lip-read without even knowing they're doing it. Test their responses when you speak without facing them.

What to do: Request a full auditory screening through your GP or the school medical service.

GENERAL ILL-HEALTH

Children who have frequent absences from school lose track of their learning, and often find it difficult to retain enough confidence to catch up.

What to watch out for: Any signs of anxiety or distress; feelings of failure or of 'not belonging' to the group or class; not wanting to go to school or to try.

What to do: Alert the class teacher to the problems. Ask for some temporary extra reading assistance to help your child regain a sense of purpose and achievement.

EMOTIONAL PROBLEMS

POOR SELF IMAGE

Children adopt all sorts of behaviour when they think they are less able than friends/siblings/peers, or they think they are less able than you expect them to be. They might give up trying altogether, telling themselves they're hopeless or useless; pretend they don't care; act aggressively – 'only wimps want to read'.

What to watch out for: Constantly putting themselves down, even in joke terms; consistently saying 'I can't' when given tasks; reluctance to try anything new because of fear of failure; feelings of inadequacy and insecurity in front of others or, conversely, attention-seeking or disruptive behaviour.

What to do: Show them that they are valued for themselves, not for what they have or can do. Give constant reassurance and encouragement. Be positive at all times in your management of them. Say, 'We'll do this together...' rather than 'You need to do...'. Say 'Good, well done!' as often as you possibly can, and stop yourself from saying 'Yes, but...'. When they compare themselves poorly with others, point out all their own good points and play down their negatives. Condition them towards positive thinking and positive self-talk. When they say, 'I'll never be able to do it,' say, 'Of course you will – we'll beat it together!' One of the best ploys you can use is to let them 'accidentally overhear' you say to an adult they respect that they are '...making tremendous progress – coming on really well...' This kind of incidental overheard remark will really increase their self-esteem and boost their motivation. They will always do their best to live up to what they secretly perceive your expectation of them to be. Be aware that it works in the negative too – if they overhear you say they're 'getting nowhere' or 'having problems' they will fulfil the prophecy. Keep reading as a role model, and encourage them to read with you. Tape stories from books and let them listen and read at the same time.

EMOTIONAL TRAUMA

Children suffer from stress as much as adults, and sometimes their stress is greater because of the confusions they feel. Bereavement, family break-ups, falling out with friends, bullying – all kinds of trauma can stop children making progress with reading. Remember, you might not know about all their traumas.

What to watch out for: Changes in behaviour. Reluctance to become involved in any activity. Depressed moods.

What to do: If you know the cause of the child's distress, alert the school and the class teacher and ask for their sympathetic understanding. Children need to talk about their feelings of loss etc. in order to come to terms with them, so encourage discussion. Look for story books which deal with the problem, read them together and talk about your responses. If the problem is not known to you, try to get them to 'open up' and talk about ways in which you might deal with it together.

LEARNING DIFFICULTIES

LANGUAGE DEPRIVATION

Children who have delayed speech, or who need a speech therapist may find reading an extremely complicated activity.

What to watch out for: Problems with speech and language will normally be picked up at a child's regular developmental check-ups and medical assistance or therapy will have been arranged. If you are worried, your first port of call should be your GP.

What to do: Encourage language development in every way you can. Do things together – but don't do all the talking! Leave gaps for your children to talk and stimulate their response.

SLOWNESS IN ALL AREAS

Where children are seen to be slow to develop in all areas of learning they may be diagnosed as having special educational needs. This is known in educational circles as 'SEN'.

What to watch out for: Any, or all, of the following might be present – short attention span, difficulty in concentrating, forgetfulness, lack of co-ordination, low self-esteem or over-confidence, very passive or disruptive behaviour, lack of interest or even total apathy.

What to do: Discuss the situation with the class teacher. Don't be too alarmed. Once a child is found to have special educational needs, a programme is set up which makes a careful and detailed assessment and the child is given the extra help that is needed. Often, the need is only temporary and a short period of individualised teaching allows the child to catch up.

DYSLEXIA
Children who experience a range of difficulties with print but who are not behind in other subjects, may be diagnosed as dyslexic or as having specific learning difficulties.

What to look out for: Difficulties with reading, writing, spelling, left-to-right orientation, co-ordination. Be aware that children can experience all of these to some extent without necessarily being dyslexic. Unfortunately, lots of parents, whose children are not doing as well as they hoped, tend to have jumped on to the dyslexia bandwagon and the condition has had a huge press. It might help to understand that dyslexia is measured on a sliding scale which we all perform on at some point, no matter how good our reading is. Therefore, it's quite possible for a child who has temporary moderate difficulties to be labelled 'dyslexic'. Many children, once they hear the word, think it's the perfect excuse not to put any effort into the task in hand so be very wary of using it!

Schools prefer the term 'specific learning difficulties'

because it necessitates a more precise diagnosis of the actual problems. Children who suffer from specific learning difficulties usually have a bizarre way of spelling – although they know the letters to write for a word, they have no idea of sequencing and get them in the wrong order. Often they rotate or reflect letters and may even do whole pages of work backwards – writing from right to left in mirror writing. They may have difficulty with sorting their right from their left. In maths they will experience difficulty with place value (tens and units), not because they do not understand the mathematical concepts, but because they muddle up the columns. This kind of confusion can only be aggravated if they are accused of being 'lazy' or 'stupid'. They don't understand why everybody else can fathom it out and they can't. Therefore, their train of thought tells them, they must be lazy or stupid, self-image plummets and the road to failure is assured.

What to do: Ask for an educational psychologist to make an assessment and diagnose the child's needs. If no help is forthcoming from the school, you can seek advice yourself from the British Dyslexia Association or the Dyslexia Institute (see page 102 for addresses).

Where specific learning difficulties are diagnosed, specialist help will be needed, and this should be provided by the school.

STATEMENTING

Where the problems are recognised to be profound the child may be 'statemented'.

Statementing involves nothing more than a very detailed assessment of the child's difficulties and needs being made by the school, usually with the involvement of other support systems, e.g. educational psychologist, speech therapist, etc. Once the assessment is made, a statement is written which specifies precisely the steps that must be taken by the school and the education authority to ensure that they provide appropriate instruction. Once the statement is written, they are under an obligation to meet the child's needs.

In severe cases, a statement may lead to a child being placed in a specialist unit (e.g. a language unit) within a mainstream school, or a special school. Again, neither of these circumstances are necessarily irretrievable – the aim is usually to get the child back into mainstream classrooms if at all possible.

WHAT YOU CAN DO TO HELP

First, don't try to cope with these difficulties alone – your GP, the school and its support services, should all be involved. Although all of the activities in this book can certainly help, real learning difficulties are not something you can, or should even try to, deal with alone. They need specific diagnosis by a trained team including an educational psychologist.

Children who have serious learning difficulties will normally have been spotted from the outset, but schools routinely allow them some time to progress at their own rate, monitoring them carefully, before taking further steps, much as you might allow and encourage them to find their own feet in physical development before consulting a physiotherapist.

Because teachers are trained always to be positive in their assessment of children, parents may not realise there is a problem. If you have any inclination at all that your children are not making any progress, then ask the teacher directly, 'Does my child have learning difficulties?' If the answer (which may be wrapped up in jargon) equates even vaguely towards 'yes' then your next question should be, 'What is the school going to do about it?'

Don't be afraid to be direct and do ask for explicit explanations of anything you do not totally understand. Remember, your child's whole future may be at stake here so it is vital that you know exactly what is happening.

WORKING WITH THE TEACHER

For your children's sake you need to strike a careful balance between being concerned and being pushy. Only a small percentage of children will fall into the groups discussed above. Most difficulties that children experience are less significant and are transitory.

As soon as you feel there may be a problem, ask to discuss it with the teacher. If it has not yet become apparent in class, she will be able to watch out for it. If the teacher agrees that it exists, ask for help in deciding the best way to tackle it. It's important that children feel their parents and teachers are working together, not against each other, so try to keep good communications open.

Be honest and open with the teacher. There's no point in promising to do back-up work if you know it's impossible to fit into your schedule. Far better that the teacher knows exactly how much support you are realistically able to give at home.

PRACTICAL ACTIVITIES

MAKE READING ENJOYABLE

* Continue to give regular help at home. Five or ten minutes every day is a fair enough aim. Allow plenty of time for the children to look through a book or story before expecting them to read to you. Work only when they are willing and try to make it fun. Stop when they've had enough.

* Carry on reading aloud to the children even when they have begun to read for themselves. Let them go back to familiar books as often as they want, to boost confidence and confirm success.

* Take care to select material that is at the right reading level, and of interest. To encourage fluency and understanding use books which link with their hobbies and interests; they need to be neither too simple (which is patronising) nor too hard (which leads to struggle).

* Continue to play reading games. Modify the activities in this book to suit the situation. For example, sometimes children learn the contents of their 'reading book' and remember the pages from the pictures, but refuse to look at the print. Make a little dictionary of words that appear in the book, or a set of flashcards showing those words

and others to do with family life. Instead of reading books, play 'Find me the word that says...' games. Give points for right answers, with a reward for a certain number of points. Play against the clock to give more challenge.

* Show confidence in their ability. Keep positive at all times; praise every achievement, however small. Hide any concern or anxiety you feel as it will communicate itself to the child and result in further loss of self-confidence.

TALK TO THE TEACHER
* If there is concern, the teacher will suggest ways for you to help. If he or she feels you are expecting too much, take the pressure off.

Be patient and tolerant. Reading is not an easy process. Miracles do not happen overnight. Stay with it!

Chapter Six

HELPING YOUR CHILD TO IMPROVE

KEEPING THEM READING

One of the great problems teachers face is that children often feel that once they can read, there's no need to carry on doing it. Somehow you have to keep them reading.

It is vital that when they reach this stage you carry on helping and encouraging them.

Reading is like any other skill – it needs constant practice. Children who spend long periods of time without reading (school holidays, for instance) can lose their skills, and they find it very difficult to catch up once they're left behind.

In a way, it's worse with reading because once the children become 'switched off' it's much harder to get them going again. They become involved in new interests or occupations. They move on quickly and you will have a fight on your hands to get them to go back.

THE READING HABIT
You cannot begin too early to introduce your children to the reading process.

Even very small babies enjoy sitting on your lap, listening to the pages turning and the sound of your voice as you read to them. Although they only see vague colours and shapes at first, gradually their visual skills will develop until they can point out things they recognise and name them. They will enjoy turning the pages for themselves and trying out the sounds they hear.

Don't think you always have to be involved, however. From a very early age children can be left with books that they can enjoy looking at by themselves, and this is to be encouraged.

Your aim should be to foster the reading habit so that it becomes second nature to them to pick up books or other reading material as eagerly as they switch on the television.

LISTENING TO THEM READ

Try to make regular, short periods of time available for listening to your children read. Turn it into a good habit for both you and for them.

Make an effort to use times when they are not distracted by other things they would rather be doing – e.g. watching television or playing with friends. Choose times when you can be relaxed and give your undivided attention. Once again, short, often and regular is much better than long and intermittent.

Sit comfortably together in an informal way, and let them feel the warmth and security of this shared period of time. In primary classrooms teachers try their hardest to set up informal reading situations with sofas, bean bags or mats to sit on. What they are trying to do is reflect a good home. They're attempting to offer a measure of comfort so that the children are conditioned to equate reading with contentment and enjoyment. You have the advantage to start with.

CHOOSE BOOKS WITH CARE

There needs to be a match of material to both the children's ability and interests. If the text is too hard they will struggle and quickly become distressed. Tension will arise between you. Suggest that you bring the session to a close and choose a different book together for next time.

If the book is too easy, they will sail happily on without paying any attention whatsoever to the content and will quickly become bored. You may get the feeling that they are not putting in any effort. Again, tension can arise which can only do damage to their attitudes towards the reading process. End the session and, together, select something more challenging for next time.

RESPONDING TO THE TEXT

Talk about the text as you go along. You should not keep up a running commentary but just make general remarks that you can discuss together, e.g.: 'That's funny, isn't it?'; 'Do you think he should do that?'; 'Let's look at the picture'; etc.

The children will react to your responses and in doing this you can get a feeling of exactly how much they are understanding and enjoying the text. The more they can talk about what they are reading or have read, the better. It means they are practising putting ideas and concepts into their own words, and working out causes, effects and hypotheses in their heads.

If they make what seem to be completely disconnected remarks – query them gently. It can mean that they are not following the text at all. Or it may be that the ideas in their books have set them off on the trail of other ideas – this kind of lateral thinking should be encouraged.

HOW YOU SHOULD COPE WITH MISTAKES

Listening to children read takes patience. You have to give them constant encouragement in order not to knock their confidence. It's very easy to get exasperated and impatient when they get words wrong.

It helps if you understand the nature of their mistakes. For instance, they may read a word correctly on one page but get it wrong on others. What they have probably done is recognise the initial letter and predict the word correctly from the meaning of the sentence they're reading in the first instance. In later instances, although they know the first sound, the meaning of the word isn't clear to them from the text.

Gently point out to them that they could 'read' the word earlier. Take them back to that text and ask them to compare the words to see if the letters match. Give them plenty of thinking time to put the word into its new context in their mind.

ACCURACY
It is very negative to insist that every word has to be read accurately. Children will often replace words with ones which have a similar meaning, e.g. 'Dad' for 'father',

'Mum' for 'mother', 'house' for 'home'.

This kind of error shows a leap from simply decoding to understanding. It means they are thinking about what they are reading and unravelling the meaning as they go along. Therefore they predict the kinds of words they would use in their own speech. Where mistakes are sensible ones, don't stop to correct them.

If, however, the guesses or predictions don't make any sense at all, this is a sign that they are so intent on decoding the words they are not aware of any sense or meaning. Take them back to the beginning of the page or the sentence. Read the words slowly with them and give the correct word without any comment.

THE DIFFICULTIES WITH 'SOUNDING OUT'

The practice of 'sounding out' is most common with children who have been taught the phonics method.

It depends on the children learning the names of the letters, and the sounds that each letter, and letter combination, makes. They then practise putting the sounds together to make words. This is called 'blending'. It works quite easily with very simple words like 'c-a-t', 'm-a-t', 'd-o-g', 'p-i-g'. But once you have exhausted the list of easy three letter words, you start to hit trouble!

There are over forty sounds in the English language, all made from a combination of 26 letters. Often the same letters produce different sounds, e.g. 'ea' as in 'head', 'ea' as in 'beat'. To be any good at sounding out, children need to be fluent in all the sounds and to be able to recognise every letter combination.

Because children's auditory discrimination skills develop at different rates you cannot always be certain they are hearing the same sound as you. Also, colds or catahrr can cause temporary hearing impairment.

Many children do not hear the 'grunting n' as in 'donkey' or the sound 'f' in (for example) 'left', or the 'r' in 'crept'. They may be unable to work out the sequence of sounds in a word like 'crisps'. Some cannot distinguish 'th' from 'v' or 's'. Vowels are pronounced differently in different regions. The 'n' in 'drink'(for example) sounds very different from the 'n' in 'nut' or 'spin'.

It is very difficult to give the sound of a letter without it being part of a word. Therefore the sounds that are described to children are often not true sounds. For example, a teacher may say that the letter 'd' says 'duh', 'o' says 'o', 'g' says 'guh' because it is almost impossible to swallow the ending of the sound. But once you try to blend the sounds duh-o-guh what you actually get is duogu not dog.

The whole business of sounding out, or blending, is a very complicated one; it's not really helpful unless you are a fairly competent reader. Try picking some long words from the dictionary at random and sounding them out for yourself. You'll find that if you didn't actually know what the words were you'd have quite a job to get them simply from blending.

If you do want to practise blending with your children, the best thing to do is to teach simple letter strings, such as 'spr', 'str', 'ing', 'ful', 'tion'. They will need good visual and auditory memory skills and a great deal of mechanical practice. Make cards with each letter string on and play matching and sorting games with them.

PROMPTING

A strategy called Pause, Prompt and Praise is more helpful, with children of all abilities. It is particularly successful with older children who are reluctant or less able readers.

The principle behind it is to make opportunities for building up reader confidence, remembering that the greatest motivating factor for children learning to read is their belief that they can do it.

When they come to a word they can't read, ask them to wait for moment and think about it. Encourage them to try identifying the word by using any strategy which works for them. For instance, they may search the pictures for a clue, or perhaps the word appeared on an earlier page. Take them back to it to see if they recognise it in a different context. If they want to have a go at sounding it out, help by breaking it into syllables or sound units with your fingers and remind them of any sounds they can't recognise. If none of these tactics work, tell them to miss it out, read on to the end of the sentence and try to work out from the meaning what it might be. If they guess it, say, 'Good. Excellent.' If they don't, give the word quietly and gently. When they repeat it, say, 'Well done,' and let them carry on.

You must allow plenty of thinking time for this.

Once children become used to PPP they soon identify their own best strategies for reading a word. Your praise is vitally important because it takes the 'failure' away. What you do is applaud them for having a go, not blame them for not recognising a word. Even though they may seem not to notice it, the praise never falls on deaf ears but adds to their feeling of confidence and self-esteem which, in turn, builds up their proficiency.

SILENT READING

Eventually children reach the point where they are quite capable of reading 'inside their heads' and this is the point at which you may begin to feel you are no longer in control.

Remember, this is what you have been aiming for. You have to trust them to actually be reading, which is quite a difficult thing to do at first. You may have all sorts of doubts about whether they're actually taking anything in or even doing what they say they're doing.

If you insist upon them reading aloud you will slow down their reading. You will also cramp their style and make them feel that you're only interested in babyish reading. They now feel themselves to be independent readers and you have to let them enjoy and develop their skills.

To check, you might ask them to tell you what they've been reading about, or what they think they've learned, but be careful not to let them think you're testing them. Far better to read the texts yourself and discuss your own responses with them. They might enjoy taking part in a lively exchange of opinions and you'll be able to gauge how well they've read.

They may also be happy to read to younger children, material that those children enjoy. Encourage them to do this – it gives them practice in pronunciation and reading with expression. They can also act as reading partners for younger children – teaching them – and this will add to their self-esteem and their skills.

GETTING AWAY FROM BOOKS

Reading, of course, isn't, and should not be, confined to books. Because it is a life-skill it's important that children understand reading is a useful tool which they must manipulate to their advantage. You can widen their reading experience easily by using the incidental material which you find all around you.

Introduce them to all kinds of different print layout. Reference books and general information sheets, for example, may be printed in columns like newspapers. Look for material with different layouts and design. Bar charts, graphs, boxes, mapping schemes – all are reading material and it's imperative that children learn how to interpret them as early as possible.

Notices, signs and labels are all around. Supermarket trips are a rich source of reading material. Don't let the children push the trolley whilst you search out the bargains – do it the other way round! This way you can get them identifying contents from labels, as well as searching out, and learning to read, brand names. It might take longer to do the shopping but it's worth it for the reading development!

Explain how the nutritional information boxes work, get them to read and compare them; get them to compare weights and measures, read advertising blurb, look out for special offers. All this is real reading experience, and might prove even more valuable than listening to them read a book from school!

Encourage them to exchange letters with friends and members of the family. Remember, a writing child is always a reading child, so the more writing they do the more they will be reading.

If there are calendar dates to make a note of, let the children do it on a communal calendar. They can check each other's, and your, notes and writing, thus adding to the reading experience.

When they bring letters and notices home from school, get the children to read them out to you whilst you're busy, rather than putting them aside to read when they've gone to bed.

Use how-to books together. Lots of books are available describing how to do things that children enjoy – making models, pop-ups, paper craft, etc. Choose a book together and follow the instructions. Let the children read and attempt to interpret the instructions to you. Only intervene if you really have to.

READING TO LEARN

Once they have become fairly fluent in reading, children are expected to use their reading skills in order to learn.

This, in turn, develops their reading ability further, along with their thinking skills.

Children work on subject areas and topics, using their literacy skills to extract information from texts and to record it. This used to mean copying huge chunks of text from books, but today they are expected to have much greater skills in processing information.

By the end of primary school children need to know how to locate information in reference books, using chapter headings, indexes, etc.; how to read maps, charts and tables; how to actually go and find something out for themselves.

The more practice they get at home, the easier they will find it in school. Find as many excuses as you can to use encyclopedias together, as well as programme listings, directories, dictionaries, manuals and text books. Teach them how to look up information and let them do it for themselves with your guidance. They may be quite slow at first, but don't be tempted to do it for them because this will only reinforce any ideas they have of it being a difficult task.

WHAT READING IS REALLY ABOUT

Four elements make up good reading. These are:
* fluency
* accuracy
* understanding
* expression

Children do not always understand this. They may think that 'good' reading is all about getting the words exactly right and nothing else. Or about reading the words without stumbling at all.

The most crucial factor is probably understanding. It is quite common for children to learn to read aloud and not have a clue what they're reading about. Their pronunciation may be perfect, but unless they can interpret the text and give it back to you in their own words, there is little point in their reading it. They are only 'barking at the print'. Imagine yourself reading a highly focused paper on a subject you know nothing about – say a medical piece full of terms and vocabulary completely strange to you. Probably you could read the paper with some fluency, accuracy and expression – but what would it mean to you?

'Barking at the print' can sometimes be a problem for children whose home language is not English – they somehow learn how the print works and the sounds it makes, but they have little idea of what it means. The best thing you can do in this case is to use English in as much verbal and written communication as you possibly can, in order to increase their proficiency in the language.

STARTING LATE

It's never too late to start helping your children with their reading. Once you show a non-judgemental interest in what they're doing, they'll begin to respond.

Sometimes, children who have managed to keep their heads above water in the primary school suddenly find they are really floundering when they move into secondary education. Your timely input can be invaluable.

There is often a huge jump in the readability level of the texts children are expected to read in secondary school. The schools take children with different levels of ability and expectation from several primarys. They have to do their best to provide for a huge range of ability. They have to buy multiple copies of the books they think will be worthwhile for most children.

Difficult books or worksheets can make for frustration and loss of confidence. To prevent this, help your children to change their reading tactics a little. Instead of reading whole pages or chapters and expecting to understand and recall information from them, they need to take in small chunks – a paragraph at a time if necessary. They should then discuss with you whether they understand the paragraph – what point is it trying to make to them? They can jot down notes for each chunk of information.

Often the language level of books and worksheets is much higher than those they have previously been used to. Not only the vocabulary will have changed, but also the sentence structure and the use of devices such as metaphors and similes. Talk these through with them. Often they can understand what the language is saying once they stop panicking and really think about, or discuss, it.

Your watchwords must be patience, tolerance and understanding. Anything that increases their frustration will make the reading so much harder and since, in the main, all higher learning depends upon reading ability, you cannot afford for them to be put off in any way.

PRACTICAL ACTIVITIES

You can boost your children's reading ability within days just by giving some concentrated attention, and getting them to co-operate with you.

KEEP A READING LOG

Enlist their help in keeping a Reading Log of everything they read over a past week. This should show the type of text, how long it took them, a comment on the reading level from them.

Use the one shown on the opposite page as an example.

READING LOG   Week beginning
                               Week ending

What I've read	How long it took	Kind of text	What I think
Charlie and the Chocolate Factory	6 days	Story	It was good
Letter from Gran	5 mins	Letter	Must write back

MAKE A READING CONTRACT

* Negotiate with them how, together, you might step up their reading programme. You will know the best ways to motivate your own children. Some children are motivated by having individual attention from a parent, others need the promise of some kind of reward. Aim to get them to agree to double the amount of reading they are doing, with your help and interest, for a short period of time – say, four days, or a week. If you try to make the period of time too long it will seem too onerous to them. Better to go for a short time, then review, then take on another chunk of time. Make a contract with them that you will be as involved in as they are – and stick to that contract. If they can see that their reading development assumes an important place in your life, then they will be willing to put in more effort.

* Set aside a time every single day when you can work together on their reading. Pick times that do not clash with their favourite TV programmes. Make sure they know when those times are to be, and what is expected of them. The important thing is that you do not deviate from your intentions. Once you let something else put you off, the reading sessions lose their importance and that will lead to loss of motivation.

* Decide together on the reading material you will use. If there are problems with homework, try not to use the same texts. If they need to get at information, use the library for reference books. Often access to books with a slightly easier text or layout than those provided by the school solve a lot of problems.

* When you have worked out all the details of your contract, write them into another log. Post it on the fridge or somewhere that neither you nor they can miss it. Then stick to it. Don't leave room for any excuses. Use all the knowledge you have learned from this book to help you to teach them. Make your sessions as enjoyable and challenging as possible. Make jokes about giving gold stars or pats on the back or house points or some other kind of reward as an incentive – and be generous!

* Check the second log against the original. Discuss it together and try to find ways where things went wrong, or where you might have stepped up the work even more. You will be amazed at the profound effect regular one-to-one concentrated attention for even short periods of time has upon reading ability.

Have a break for a couple of days, then negotiate another contract.

This is particularly crucial during school holiday periods when skills not used very easily degenerate. Build upon them instead!

Chapter Seven

HOW WELL DOES YOUR CHILD READ?

TESTING IN SCHOOLS

In school, children's reading is measured by testing.

There are basically three kinds of tests:
* standardised assessment tests
* diagnostic tests
* S.A.T.S.

STANDARDISED ASSESSMENT TESTS

These give the teacher a 'Reading Age'. These tests are designed by educational experts and tested vigorously nationwide before they are sold to schools.

Creating tests is a difficult art. Test writers cannot pluck a norm out the air and say, 'This is what you must do to have a Reading Age of eight.' They have to work on the principle that if they devise twenty questions and the majority of eight-year-olds score eighteen – then all children scoring eighteen on the test can be said to have a Reading Age of eight. If, in their trials, the majority of eight-year-olds scored between five and ten they would have to rewrite the test because it would be proved to be too difficult for the average eight-year-old.

You can see from this that a Reading Age is not at all comparable with a chronological age. All a Reading Age really shows you is whether your child is average, below or above (compared with the children who took part in the trials) – at the time of testing. There can be problems with adminstering the tests. Many things can influence the scores. For instance, a child having a bad day for any reason will not score well on a standardised reading test. Well-being and emotions can make a difference. Best performances aren't forthcoming from children with colds or tummy-aches, or upsets because they've just fallen out with their friends.

Prior knowledge can effect scores. For example, if the content of the test is Greek Gods and the children happen to have already done a project on Greek Gods then some of the vocabulary and concepts will be familiar to them so they may score better than with a completely unknown text.

There are different commercial tests, the schools choose which ones they will buy. It is quite possible for children to attain different scores on different tests, resulting in totally different Reading Ages.

DIAGNOSTIC TESTS
These are written specifically to pinpoint particular problems, e.g. visual or auditory discrimination, orientation, sequencing, etc. They are normally only given to individual children who are not making enough progress. They allow the teacher to work out what specific problems the children have and what they can do to help them.

S.A.T.S.
SATS (Standard Assessment Tasks) are a requirement of

the National Curriculum. Children are assessed at the ages of seven, eleven, fourteen and sixteen, at the end of each Key Stage.

There are six Levels of reading attainment (see page 106) for Key Stages 1 and 2. Each Level of Attainment has several statements of what children should be able to do to achieve that Level. Most seven-year-old children should be at Level 2; most eleven-year-olds should achieve Level 4.

Children who are between Levels are said to be working towards the next Level and the teacher must provide them with work which will allow them to achieve all of the targets in that Level.

SATS are quite complex for teachers to administer, because they are time-consuming and the children have to be given individual attention. The tests are really still in the process of being developed so it's not possible to detail their formats as these may be changed from year to year, though it can be generally assumed that the pattern will need to be some kind of test of comprehension.

WHAT DO TESTS INVOLVE?

The only way that reading ability can really be tested is by trying to get at the understanding the children have of what they have read.

This usually involves them in some kind of comprehension test.

COMPREHENSION TESTING
A comprehension test can be conducted verbally or on

paper. Because of the number of children involved in a classroom, comprehension tests are most often on paper. There will be a text and perhaps an illustration, followed by a set of questions. The children have to read and understand the text, then read, understand and answer the questions.

The basic flaw with comprehension tests is that children may understand perfectly what the question is asking them and what the answer should be, but if their reading and writing abilities are at odds (and writing ability is almost always behind reading ability) – they may not be able to write down the answers in a coherent way. When their answer papers are marked are they really being marked for reading competence or writing ability?

For this reason, tests usually also involve multiple choice questioning, and Cloze Procedure. (These are explained below, under the heading 'How can you help prepare them?').

HOW CAN EXAM TECHNIQUE HELP?

If you think about it, even GCSEs are almost a kind of comprehension test. They require children to read and understand, to listen and understand, to do practical activities and understand. The children are then expected to demonstrate their understanding. They are more likely to be asked to write an essay demonstrating their understanding, and thus knowledge, rather than given a series of twenty questions – but the basic concept is still the same.

This is why it is said that you should learn exam technique in order to pass exams. Exam technique is all about understanding what the question is getting at and answering it in the most appropriate way to demonstrate your own understanding.

Once children perceive that it is their ability to demonstrate understanding, rather than they as a person that is being tested, they are well on the way towards success and achievement.

IS TESTING REALLY NECESSARY?

Most teachers will be able to tell you exactly how much progress your children are making, from day-to-day observation of their work.

At its best, assessment testing usually tells them something they already know – that one reader is more fluent or less fluent than another. At its worst it can fill a parent or a child with panic, encourage unhealthy competition and put undue pressure on the learner.

Many teachers do not believe that Reading Ages or Levels of Attainment are really true indicators of a child's development. Many feel it is unrealistic to measure one child's competence against another's, in the same way that it would be impractical to compare their physical growth.

HOW SHOULD YOU LOOK AT TESTING?

The best way to approach testing, or examinations, as a parent, is to treat it as a fact of life that it is better to prepare your children for, than to ignore.

The very word 'test' can strike fear into the heart of those with low self esteem, they see themselves as failing before they even begin. Your task is really to get them to view it in a different way.

Explain to them gently that a test is not there to prove that they can't do it, but to help them upgrade themselves towards the next step. If they have plenty of time to understand what is expected of them, they won't find it such a difficult experience. If they have practised a few times with you, they will have a much more positive attitude.

HOW CAN YOU HELP TO PREPARE THEM?

All comprehension tests require that readers can read the text, and can also read between the lines. They are asked literal questions, the answers to which can always be found in the text, and they are asked questions which require them to make inferences or deductions for themselves from the text, thus proving their total understanding.

Example: *John and Mary had a picnic in the park. John had packed meat sandwiches. "Yuk!" said Mary. The geese loved them.*

A literal question would be: What did John and Mary do in the park? Answer: They had a picnic. The text states this explicitly.

An inferential question would be: What did Mary do with her sandwiches? Why? Answer: She gave them to the geese because she didn't like meat. You have to deduce this from the text.

You can get children used to increasing their understanding and expectations of texts simply by sharing discussion when you're reading together. Ask questions: why, what, how, when, where, do you think? Encourage them to extend their thinking past exactly what they have read.

At the end of the story, ask which part the children liked best, what might happen if the story continued, what did they think of the characters' actions, how would they have felt if... etc. etc.

You can have the same kind of discussion over reference material. In particular, make sure that they can read the information that is stated in tables, charts and graphs. Say: 'From this chart can we tell if...', 'Can we use this map to compare...?" and so on.

Modify this approach to suit children embarking upon GCSEs. Help them to study their subjects and discuss with you exactly what knowledge they have. Although it's valuable to ask them questions to prompt instant recall, it's also necessary for them to practise putting those answers down on paper. Children who are knowledgeable but lost when it comes to writing things down score much lower in exams. As with reading, in writing practice is the important thing.

Multiple choice questioning will usually have, in the early stages of reading at least, three or four statements. The reader chooses which one is correct to tick or circle. Sometimes the testers use almost trick statements, just to make sure that the child is following the pattern of thinking in the text. For instance, a multiple choice question on our text might read:

Example: *John and Mary had a picnic in the park. John had packed meat sandwiches. "Yuk!" said Mary. The geese loved them.*

What did the geese do? Tick the right answer.

They swam on the pond.

They ate the meat sandwiches.

They pecked John's fingers.

You can see that, although all of the statements might be correct in a child's imagination of what happened at the park, there is only one correct statement as far as the text is concerned.

To prepare the children for this kind of multiple choice question, make up your own questions from the texts that you share with them. Turn the questioning into a game, making your questions as much fun as possible, and guide them to see that only a statement which pertains to the actual text scores points. So, for Humpty Dumpty, for instance you could ask them, 'Is Humpty a soldier?', 'Is Humpty an egg?' 'Does Humpty roll down hills?' 'Did Humpty get broken?'. The more practice they get at eliminating the things that could be right but which are not actually in the text, the better they will perform at multiple choice questioning.

Cloze Procedure works in a different way. It leaves gaps in sentences which the children have to fill in. Although this sounds simple, it actually shows a high order of understanding because the words that are omitted from the text are often particular parts of speech, perhaps nouns, pronouns, adverbs, adjectives. The child is obliged to understand the whole sentence and its context in order to discern which kind of word needs to be inserted.

A Cloze Procedure piece on our text might read:

Example: *John and Mary had a picnic in the park. John had packed meat sandwiches. "Yuk!" said Mary. The geese loved them.*

Fill in the missing words:

John and Mary _ _ _ _ having a picnic _ _ the park when lots of geese _ _ _ _ up to them. The children threw _ _ _ _ meat sandwiches to them. The geese _ _ _ _ _ _ _ the sandwiches _ _ .

For scoring, other words than the exact ones the tester has in mind may be used, as long as they are the correct part of speech. A child who wrote 'park' instead of 'were' or 'to' instead of 'in' or 'at' would be showing at best problems with syntax and sequencing, at worst non-comprehension of the piece. Because of the way children's minds work they might easily see the phrase 'having a picnic', relate it to 'park', see that the gap has four spaces, and so put the word in. Their minds could also read '— the park' as 'they went to the park', and so they would write in 'to'. But what their misconceptions are showing is that they have a complete misunderstanding of how the language of the text works. Therefore, their reading ability is not fluent.

You can easily practise Cloze Procedure exercises at home by writing letters and stories together and asking the child to predict the word that is going to come next. Or by taking words out of stories, rhymes, poems etc. and asking them which words they could use in the space. Make it fun, make jokes about words that couldn't possibly fit in, make them really think about what comes next. Again, lots of informal practice will ensure success in formal testing.

READING AND WRITING

At any stage of development there is a strong connection between reading and writing. Writing is to reading as speaking is to listening.

In the early stages, try not to worry too much about handwriting and spelling. What you are after is the ability of the children to communicate their ideas, thoughts and feelings on paper. Much as you learn to understand what they are saying when they first start to talk, you should try and track what they are writing. Gradually with help and positive encouragement their skills will develop.

Remember, always, that children who develop good speaking and listening skills will have far greater success in literacy activities than children with a poor facility for language.

Teachers' Reports

Although teachers' reports exist to give some evaluation of the children's progress, they are not as easy to write as you may think. To begin with, teachers, on the whole, are trained to work towards the positive. This is with good reason. They cannot be in the home of every child to know what kind of response a poor report will elicit from an irate parent. Also, they know very well that the last thing children with low self esteem need is more negative feedback.

So, even though he may be trailing miserably behind his Level 3 peers, the teachers will write in as positive a way as possible: e.g. 'Tom is working well towards Level 2', or 'Tom has learned all the initial sounds' when, to be on a level with his peers he really should be miles past them.

Because of this tendency towards positivity, parents often say they had no idea their children were in any way struggling or behind. The only way to counteract it is to be present on Parents' Nights and to actually talk with the teacher. If it is impossible to make the fixed interview, then it is your right to ask for an appointment that fits in with your own timetable.

Ask direct questions. If the response to, 'How is Tom doing with reading?' is, 'He's on Level 2' – ask what that means in terms of the rest of the children in the class. Ask, 'Is he holding his own?', 'Is he making good progress?', 'Is he struggling?', 'Is there something specific I can help him with?', 'How can I become involved?' Focused questions will usually evoke a straight answer.

PARENTS' MEETINGS

Children are always excited and frightened about Parents' Meetings. They want to know exactly how you got on, and what the teacher said about them. Their main fear is never that their work is 'no good', but that their teacher doesn't like them. They are also afraid that you might say something which will queer their pitch with the teacher!

Be as open as you can with them, tell them a little of the discussion and if there are any negative things to be said, try and say them in a positive way. Rather than 'She said you're miles behind with reading', say 'She's told me about some games we can play together to help you with your reading'.

Every Moment Is a Learning Moment

You can do so much to expand your children's under-standing, and their language development just by spend-ing the time to converse with them. Every single moment of a child's life is a learning moment, whether you want it to be or not! Good parents take every opportunity to expand their children's world through ordinary events – shopping trips, picnics, visiting, watching television together – even cleaning the house together! Throughout all of these activities you can be talking with them and lis-tening to them, to increase the language ability that will have enormous effects upon their reading development.

THEY HAVE TO EXPERIMENT.
All language learning involves making errors as well as being correct. Children need to feel safe to try out new ideas and strategies, secure in the knowledge that they won't be criticised or laughed at if they make a mistake. Let them experiment with their speaking and writing, and they will flourish.

A Family Affair

Promote literacy as a family affair. This doesn't mean one member of the family taking total responsibility. It means everyone joining in. Spend time, rather than money, talk-ing to your children, encouraging and furthering their interests. Every time you pay a bill, look up a phone number, write a shopping list, discard the junk mail, etc. you are presenting a literacy model to them. This doesn't mean that you have to make it a focus of attention, but try to make it something that they accept as a normal part of real family life, not something that you do when they're not there.

NURTURE THEIR LITERACY ACHIEVEMENTS

Try to ensure, particularly in the later years, that your children have a quiet place where they can do their reading and writing without being disturbed. This doesn't necessarily have to mean a room of their own, but it's important to create some zone in the house that is as free from noise and distraction as possible – even if it's a corner under the stairs. Try to furnish the zone with bookshelves, some kind of desk and a variety of materials for writing and reading. Felt tip pens, pencils, erasers, paper, magazines, comics, scrapbooks, etc. will all help to enhance this study area.

If this isn't a possibility, keep a box full of materials in an easily accessed place, perhaps in the kitchen, and let the kitchen table become the workspace. While you're doing the domestic bit, let them be being writers and readers.

It's also useful to keep a small bag of reading and writing materials in the car for use on trips and visits.

Your response, of course, is all important. A child who has written a spontaneous letter to Gran doesn't want to be told that it has lots of spelling mistakes but to receive a letter back saying how full of joy Gran is to hear from them. It's the message that's important and the fact that they can see you understand that. If they are criticised at every turn they will very easily be put off.

Stories and pictures stuck on to the fridge, the freezer, the garage wall, should be read avidly – and enjoyed!

THE KEY TO SUCCESS

Parents are a child's first teachers. Research has shown, over and over again, that the children of parents who model good literacy patterns in the home, generally raise children who become successful literacy learners.

It is not exaggerating to say that the golden key to success in reading, for your children, is – YOU!

GLOSSARY

The following are some of the subject-specific terms that teachers or books might use, with simplified explanations. All of these terms are used in this book.

Apprenticeship reading
Child and adult read together, with adult leading. A kind of 'sitting next to Nellie' learning.

Auditory discrimination
Sorting out differences in sound.

Barking at the print
Reading fluently without any understanding.

Blending
Putting the sounds of specific letter units together to form different sounds.

Breakthrough to Literacy
A commercial programme of the Language Experience strategy.

Cloze Procedure
A device for testing understanding – children fill in the missing words.

Colour coding
A system of grading books according to difficulty.

Context Support
A strategy for teaching reading whereby children hear a long version of the text before reading an abridged one.

Diagnostic Tests
Tests for specific problems, administered to individuals. Performance in diagnostic tests helps teachers decide what course of action to take.

Dyslexia
An umbrella term for certain reading problems.

Emergent reader
One who is just beginning to flourish.

ERIC
Everyone Reading In Class – a strategy for quiet reading periods.

Holistic Language
See Whole Language.

Individualised reading
A programme by which all resource books, reading scheme books and real books, are categorised into thirteen different reading levels.

Key Stages
National Curriculum is organised on the basis of four key stages, which are, broadly:
Key Stage 1 5 – 7 years
Key Stage 2 7 – 11 years
Key Stage 3 11 – 14 years
Key Stage 4 14 – 16 years

Language Experience
A strategy by which children write their own texts and read them back. See Breakthrough to Literacy.

Letterland
A commercial pictogram programme.

Look and say
A method by which children learn to recognise individual whole words.

Multiple choice
A technique for questioning, where children are given several options from which to choose the correct one.

Orientation
The way the print should be read on a page – i.e. in English, from left to right, from top to bottom.

Pause, prompt and praise
A strategy for listening to reading and encouraging prediction skills.

Phonics
A method which concentrates on letters and their sounds.

Place value
A mathematical term for numerical columns.

Readability level
The language level of a text.

Reading methods
Techniques used to teach children to read.

Reading schemes
Books with controlled and graded texts, written with the specific aim of enabling children to read.

Real books
All books which are not part of a reading scheme.

S.A.T.S.
Standardised Assessment Tests. These are government controlled, required by National Curriculum. The test results give a Level which the child has achieved in National Curriculum terms.

Self image
How a learner sees himself, in terms of personality, success and failure.

Sequencing
Getting things in the right order – these can be letters, words, sounds, concepts in a story.

Sounding out
Breaking words into small parts, and trying to work them out from putting the sounds of the parts together. See Blending.

Specific Learning Difficulties
Serious problems with reading. Educationalists find this term more helpful than 'dyslexia' because it assumes a need to make a very detailed assessment and find out exactly what problems are present.

Standardised Tests
Apart from SATS, schools may use their own choice of

standardised tests which measure ability against average norms.

Statementing
A child with special needs will be fully assessed by the school and by outside support agencies. A Statement will then be written which will show exactly what needs the child has, and how they will be fulfilled by the school and the local education authority.

USSR
Uninterrupted, silent, sustained reading. A strategy for quiet reading periods.

Visual discrimination
Sorting out differences in appearance.

Whole language
A way of teaching the language which focuses on all of the communication skills together rather than seeing them as separate facilities.

Word attack skills
Strategies for tackling unfamiliar words.

USEFUL ADDRESSES

The British Dyslexia Association
98 London Road,
Reading,
Berks RG1 5AU
Tel: 01734 668271

The Dyslexia Institute
133 Gresham Road,
Staines,
Middlesex TW18 2AJ
Tel: 01784 463851

The Children's Book Foundation
Book Trust
45 East Hill,
London SW18 2QZ
Tel: 0181 870 9055

The Irlen Centre
4 Moscow Mansions,
224 Cromwell Road,
London SW5 0SP
Tel: 0171 244 7099

The Reading and Language Information Centre
University of Reading,
Bulmershe Court,
Earley,
Reading RG6 1HY
Tel: 01734 318820

APPENDIX 1

PHONIC SOUNDS (see Chapter Two, Practical Activities)
The following is a list of all the phonic sounds which are
taught in the phonic method. You can see there's a lot to
learn!

Initial Single Consonants
t, b, n, r, m, s, d, c (hard as in 'cat'), p, g (hard as in 'goat')
f, l, y, v, h, w, j, k, z

Doubled Consonants
bb, dd, ff, gg, etc. and ck

Initial Consonant Digraphs (a digraph is two letters which
combine to make one sound)
ch, sh, th (as in three), wh, th (as in 'that', qu)

Initial Consonant Blends (a blend is bringing sounds
together)
st, sp, sc, sk, sl, sm, sn, sw,
br, cr, dr, pr, tr, gr, fr,
bl, pl, cl, fl, gl

Short vowels
(i) Initial sounds
a as in 'apple', i as in 'ink', e as in 'egg
o as in 'orange', u as in 'umbrella'
(ii) Medial sounds
a as in 'bat', i as in 'tin', e as in 'pet'
o as in 'hot', u as in 'bug'
(iii) Final sounds
y as in 'baby'
y as in 'fly'

Vowel digraphs
ai, ay, oi, oy,
oo (as in 'wood' and 'food')
oa, ow (as in 'cow' and 'snow'), ou, (as in 'about' and 'rough')
au, aw, al
ee, ea (as in 'bean' and 'head')
ew, ue
ei,
ie

Other sounds for c, g, s
c followed by e, i, or y
g followed by e, i, or y (sounds like 'j')
s makes the 'z' sound as in 'has'

Final e
Silent as in 'kettle' 'noise' 'jumble'
Works as 'magic e' in cake, bite, bone, cube

Modification of vowels by r
ar as in 'car' 'for' 'sister'
ir as in 'girl', ur as in 'burn'

Silent letters
b, g, m, gh, k, l, p, t, w

Prefixes
ab, ad, be, com, de, dis, en, ex, pro, re, sub

Suffixes
ing, ed, er, ly, es, tion, y

Syllables
ion, tion, sion, ation, er, y, al, ent, ful, ity, ly, ure, ous

APPENDIX 2
(see Chapter Three, Practical Activities)

Different schools may use slightly different styles but if you keep the letters clear like this – don't join them up – you will be on the right lines.

a b c d e

f g h i j k

l m n o p

q r s t u v

w x y z

APPENDIX 3
(see Chapter Seven)

THE NATIONAL CURRICULUM ATTAINMENT TARGET FOR READING (KS1/KS2)

LEVEL 1
Pupils recognise familiar words in simple texts. They use their knowledge of letters and sound-symbol relationships in order to read words and to establish meaning when reading aloud. In these activities they sometimes require support. They express their response to poems, stories and non-fiction by identifying aspects they like.

LEVEL 2
Pupils' reading of simple texts shows understanding and is generally accurate. They express opinions about major events or ideas in stories, poems and non-fiction. They use more than one strategy, such as phonic, graphic, syntactic and contextual, in reading unfamiliar words and establishing meaning.

LEVEL 3
Pupils read a range of texts fluently and accurately. They read independently, using strategies appropriately to establish meaning. In responding to fiction and non-fiction they show understanding of the main points and express preferences. They use their knowledge of the alphabet to locate books and find information.

LEVEL 4
In responding to a range of texts, pupils show understanding of significant ideas, themes, events and charac-

ters, beginning to use inference and deduction. They refer to the text when explaining their views. They locate and use ideas and information.

LEVEL 5
Pupils show understanding of a range of texts, selecting essential points and using inference and deduction where appropriate. In their responses, they identify key features, themes and characters, and select sentences, phrases and relevant information to support their views. They retrieve and collate information from a range of sources.

LEVEL 6
In reading and discussing a range of texts, pupils identify different layers of meaning and comment on their significance and effect. They give personal responses to literary texts, referring to aspects of language, structure and themes in justifying their views. They summarise a range of information from different sources.

Other books for parents by Piccadilly Press:

SPELLING FOR PARENTS
by Jo Phenix and Doreen Scott-Dunne

English spelling isn't as difficult or illogical as it seems,
once you understand it. Entertaining and easy to read,
this practical guide for parents wanting to help their
children to spell includes:

• an explanation of children's spelling development
• how to recognise children's strengths and weaknesses
• discussing children's progress effectively with teachers
• fascinating spelling trivia (did you know that William
Caxton's 'u' didn't work very well, so he changed it to
'o' in words like done and wonder?)

*'...offers refreshingly easy strategies for parents to use with
children encountering difficulties with spelling...An optimistic
book which would also be useful to adults with spelling
problems'* – The Independent

GRAMMAR FOR PARENTS
by Jerry George, with Clare Stuart

This is essential for any parent who wants to help their
child with grammar. It includes: clear definitions of the
terms we use to talk about grammar; explanations and
examples of the major rules; suggestions for using grammar creatively to improve writing; and a list of the main
grammar pitfalls.

ARE YOU EXPECTING TOO MUCH FROM YOUR CHILD?
by Dr Fiona Subotsky

Do you spend a great deal of time worrying about your child? Have you ever considered that your aims may be beyond the reach or perhaps beyond the interest of your child? Do you notice family traits in your child?

Every child deserves to be accepted for who they are not what their parents want them to be. In this book, Fiona Subotsky draws parents' attention to their own behaviour and expectations, which might have a negative effect on their child's development.

Coming soon:

MATHS FOR PARENTS
by Rosemary Russell

At last – a book for parents who want to help their children with maths but have shied away for fear of confusing them further!

Rosemary Russell discusses the different methods used in teaching maths in schools today. She explains how to build both your own, and your child's, confidence in maths; gives games you can play with your child to improve their maths without them even knowing; and what the National Curriculum means.

WELL DONE!
by Ken Adams

Your child can't be brilliant at everything! Most children have an area of weakness – verbal, mathematical or conceptual. Identify your child's weaknesses and help your child strengthen skills in these areas – without him or her even knowing.

Find out: how children learn, how they fail, specific difficulties arising in children up to the age of eleven and what you can do to help them.